King Oscar's Gamble
Sweden's Secret Plan to Attack Russia in 1856

GABRIEL STEIN

Copyright © Gabriel Stein

The right of Gabriel Stein to be identified as the author of this work has been asserted by him in accordance with the Copyright, Designs and Patents Act, 1988.

First published in 2018
ISBN: 9781790691975

CONTENTS

Introduction
Chapter 1
   The Baltic until 1852
Chapter 2: 1853: The Neutrality Declaration
Chapter 3: 1854: 1st Baltic Expedition and failed negotiations
Chapter 4: 1855: 2nd Baltic Expedition and the November Treaty
Chapter 5: Conclusion
Acknowledgements
Bibliography
A: Primary sources, unpublished
B: Primary Sources, published
   C: Secondary Sources
Appendices
   Appendix 1 – The November Treaty
   Appendix 2 – Secret article proposed by Baron Stierneld
   Appendix 3 – Draft offensive treaty
   Appendix 4 – King Oscar's plan for the 1856 campaign
The Baltic

KING OSCAR'S GAMBLE

Introduction

The Crimean War is one of the forgotten wars of British history. Most people might, if pressed, remember the Charge of the Light Brigade and Florence Nightingale. Some (notably if they are Flashman enthusiasts) may also recall the Charge of the Heavy Brigade and the Thin Red Line. But even for these cognoscenti the war remains confusing, both why and where it was fought. As W.C. Sellar and R.J Yeatman put it in *1066 and All That*, "*The French* though that the *Holy Places* ought to be guarded (probably against the *Americans*) by *Latin Monks*, while the *Turks*, who owned the Places, thought that they ought to be guarded by *Greek Monks*. *England* therefore quite rightly declared war on *Russia*, who immediately occupied *Roumania*."[i] The amount of truth in this description partly explains why the war appears so confusing.

This forgetfulness is regrettable. The Crimean War was important for a number of reasons. The ostensible origin of the war was a dispute between France and Russia about the ownership of the Holy Places in Palestine and the protection of the Christian minorities. But the war was also about such diverse issues as protecting the territorial integrity of the Ottoman Empire, maintaining the balance of power in Europe, setting a limit to Russia's expansion and revising the 1815 post-Napoleonic settlement in Europe. It was also the first war between major European powers since the end of the Napoleonic Wars and – in terms of major powers involved (four) – the largest war in Europe between 1815 and 1914. In addition to the major issues already mentioned, the war touched upon a large number of secondary issues, such as German and Italian unification, the situation in the Balkans, the Polish question, the right of neutrals (a point which became particularly important for the Scandinavian countries)[ii], the question of Liberalism vs. the Holy Alliance; and so on. All these reasons should make the Crimean War somewhat more Memorable (to use the terminology of Sellar & Yeatman).

If the Crimean War is a forgotten war, the Baltic Theatre is one of the forgotten theatres of the war. Given the natural and necessary concentration on the Crimea and on Sevastopol, that is perhaps understandable. Nevertheless, the Baltic Campaigns of 1854 and 1855 were significant and carried the potential to be considerably more important. (It was also, as it happens, the scene for the earliest action to win a Victoria Cross, namely Charles David Lucas' hurling a live but unexploded Russian shell from HMS *Hecla* into the sea during the bombardment of Bomarsund on 21st June 1854.) Throughout the war, there were attempts by the Allied governments to bring Sweden into the war, with the November Treaty of 1855 an important step in this direction. This thesis studies these negotiations and their potential consequences. Specifically, the questions addressed are the following:

Were the negotiations serious – on both sides? In other words, were the Allied governments serious in their attempts to bring Sweden into the war; or were the negotiations merely intended to divert the Russian government's attention – and perhaps also troops and other resources from the Crimea? From the Swedish side, was Sweden seriously considering joining the war? Or was the King trying to stall in a situation where he wanted to avoid having to take sides, and so setting his conditions for joining so high that they could never be met?

Was a Swedish participation in the war realistic? What this means here is, did Sweden have the financial and military resources to take an active part in the war and to contribute to the Allied strength?

If Sweden had participated in the war, what could it have contributed? This question is related to the previous one. Essentially, it asks, what could Swedish participation have achieved, militarily and/or politically and was any of it achieved without active Swedish participation?

Finally, why was it that the protracted negotiations, at one point or other actively pursued by Britain, by France and by the King of Sweden & Norway, never led to Swedish participation in the war?

The limited interest shown in the Baltic Campaign by British historians means that the question of the Baltic operations as well as the negotiations with Sweden only have been cursorily covered in English. Alexander William Kinglake's magisterial eight-volume work on the Crimean War, *The Invasion of the Crimea: Its origin and an account of its progress down to the death of Lord Raglan* only mentions the Baltic once, referring to the British public's desire for glory in that theatre.[iii] Winston Churchill barely mentions the Baltic Campaign in his description of the Crimean War in his *History of the English-Speaking Peoples*, just noting that there were two minor naval expeditions to the Baltic.[iv] Saul David mentions it once in *Victoria's Wars*, in an aside where he quotes Lord Clarendon, the British Foreign Secretary explaining the lack of winter equipment for the Crimea with a reference to needs in the Baltic.[v] Trevor Royle does discuss the negotiations between the Allies and the Swedish court in *Crimea – The Great Crimean War 1854-1856*– but (judging by his bibliography) Royle has not consulted any Swedish language sources and is from time to time sloppy and wrong about his facts.[vi] He is certainly wrong about the attitude of the Swedish King, who he claims was not prepared to jeopardise his good relations with Russia.[vii] As will be shown, the King's attitude is a critical issue and the key to the Swedish attitude during the war. John Curtiss, who writes from a Russian perspective, touches more upon the issue in *Russia's Crimean War*; but Curtiss is also prone to factual mistakes (eg, mixing up Crown Prince Karl of Sweden with his brother and successor Prince Oscar, or claiming that Sir Colin Campbell died in an assault on the Malakoff redoubt).[viii] More importantly, Curtiss, like Royle, portrays King Oscar as being against Swedish participation in the war.[ix] In Curtiss' opinion, the King deliberately set his price for participation high in order to avoid joining the war, without the need for an outright rejection.[x] This unwillingness is partly ascribed to an unwillingness to challenge a powerful neighbour; and partly to the pro-Russian attitudes of the Finns, a key issue since one of Sweden's demands was the return of Finland.[xi] David Wetzel's

The Crimean War: A Diplomatic History, only touches on the negotiations with Sweden in passing, somewhat surprisingly claiming that the resumption of talks in late 1855 and the conclusion of the November Treaty was due to the influence of the French Ambassador to London, the Duc de Persigny, on the French Emperor.[xii] This version is not encountered elsewhere and is in fact contradicted by most of the evidence. By contrast, Winfried Baumgart devotes considerable space on the non-belligerent powers in *The Crimean War 1853-1856*. On Sweden, Baumgart notes that "In view of the Allied war aim to reduce Russian power in European affairs ... Sweden's role in the war obviously seemed essential to Allied war-planners."[xiii] Baumgart also gives an overview of the negotiations between Sweden and the Allied powers, including the signing of the November Treaty. In contrast to Royle and Curtiss, he also makes it clear that King Oscar was keen on entering the war, noting that by 1855, the King's price for joining had come down; and that in 1856 he actively promoted an offensive alliance with the Allied powers.[xiv] However, he portrays the negotiations between Sweden and the Allies as if the Allies were generally acting and Sweden reacting.[xv] As this thesis will show, this was indeed the case in 1854; but by 1855, the pace was very much driven by Swedish eagerness for an alliance. J B Conacher also goes into the negotiations with Sweden in some depth in *Britain and the Crimea: Problems of War and Peace*. Conacher's account is relevant as he is one the few authors to cover, if briefly, the shifting British attitudes towards the negotiations with the Scandinavian Kingdoms.

Other authors give more attention to the Baltic. In *The Crimean War: British Grand Strategy 1853-1856* Alan Lambert declares that, rather than a sideshow, this was the second major theatre of the war.[xvi] For instance, Lambert claims that the British ultimatum to Russia was timed to expire at the earliest date that a British squadron could reach Reval.[xvii] However, Lambert's account is also marred by factual errors, eg claiming that the Treaty of Fredrikshamn in 1809 specified that the Åland islands were not to be fortified;[xviii] or that the Russian government's response to the Swedish Declaration of Neutrality included a demand for Swedish ports to be garrisoned by Russian troops.[xix] He also claims that King Oscar at various times during the war raised his price for Swedish participation.[xx] In fact, as will be shown, with one minor exception (see p. 58) the King held steadily to the conditions first enunciated in the summer of 1854 until late 1855/early 1856, when he abandoned some of them. Finally, Basil Greenhill and Ann Giffard concentrate exclusively on the war in the Baltic in their book *The British Assault on Finland 1854-1844 – A Forgotten Naval War*. Greenhill & Giffard show that a naval war with Russia almost by default meant a Baltic Campaign and that this was understood by the British Cabinet well before the war.[xxi] They also make the crucial point that following the fall of Sevastopol, there was little the Allies could do in the Crimea. If they advanced, their lines of communication lengthened, while Russia's shortened. If they did nothing, their forces would eventually have to be withdrawn. If so, Russia would soon retake the Crimea, and rebuild Sevastopol and their Black Sea fleet. Therefore, the Baltic by default became the focal point of potentially continued war.[xxii] Werner Mosse's *The Rise and Fall of the Crimean System 1855-71* looks mainly at the aftermath of the war, but also discusses the peace negotiations. Strangely, Mosse claims that the November Treaty was accompanied by an exchange of notes detailing how it was to be converted into an offensive alliance against Russia, a point repeated by Axel Jonasson in his article *The Crimean War, the Beginning of Strict Swedish Neutrality and the Myth of Swedish Intervention in the Baltic*.[xxiii] Neither gives any source, but this idea seems to emanate from self-aggrandizing statements by General Canrobert.[xxiv] Edgar Anderson's two short articles, *The Crimean War in the Baltic Area* and *The Scandinavian Area and the Crimean War in the Baltic* concentrate on the Baltic Theatre and on the political developments, both between Sweden and the Allies and in Russia. Again, however, the account suffers from factual errors: Anderson refers to Lord John Russell as Sir John;[xxv] claims that Britain sent a naval expedition to the Baltic in February 1856[xxvi] (highly unlikely, both because the ice would not have broken and because the Paris Peace Conference was well under way by then); and also that Kronstadt was besieged in 1854, a claim not encountered anywhere else.[xxvii]

One point where almost all English-language writers – Anderson, Baumgart, Curtiss, Greenhill & Giffard, Lambert and Mosse[xxviii] – tend to agree is that the November Treaty and the threat of Swedish (as well as potentially Austrian) participation in the war against Russia, played a major role in hastening the end of the Crimean War. But even here, there is a divergence between those - Curtiss, Greenhill & Giffard and Mosse[xxix] – who claim that there were secret clauses in the November Treaty paving the way for Sweden to go to war; and those who make no such mention. Lambert does note that Russia believed there were secret clauses to the Treaty, but refutes their existence by making the point that there would then have been no need to discuss an offensive treaty – as was actually being done.[xxx] This thesis will show that Lambert is right, by publishing for the first time a draft offensive Treaty drawn up in King Oscar's own handwriting – although never presented to his putative alliance partners.

Unsurprisingly, the Swedish coverage is rather more extensive. The earliest analytical writing on the topic seems to be Albin Cullberg's two-volume *La Politique du roi Oscar I pendant la guerre de Crimée* (*The policy of King Oscar I during the Crimean War*), published 1912. Cullberg feels that although King Oscar did want Sweden to participate in the war, he never would have moved had the Emperor Nicholas not died.[xxxi] He also feels that the pressure for an alliance generally came from the Allies.[xxxii] Above all, he notes that King Oscar, although a prudent diplomat, lacked the eye for the main chance. Hence he only seriously prepared for war at a time when the Allies were already moving towards peace.[xxxiii] The negotiations were further explored in both Sweden and Finland during the inter-war period, with Carl Hallendorff's *Konung Oscar I:s politik under Krimkriget* (*King Oscar I's policy during the Crimean War*) from 1930, as well as his

Oskar I, Napoleon och Nikolaus – Ur diplomaternas privatbrev under Krimkriget (*Oscar I, Napoleon and Nicholas – from the private letters of diplomats during the Crimean War*) from 1918. Both of these contain large numbers of reprinted original documents, including letters, excerpts from King Oscar's diary and other notes as well as diplomatic reports. Hallendorff's view is that the King was pro-Allied from the start and therefore ready to give up Sweden's neutrality.[xxxiv] Like other writers, he highlights the King's disappointment at the news of Russia's acceptance of the Austro-Allied terms in January 1856.[xxxv] The internal Swedish debate prior to and during the war is covered by Sven Eriksson, *Svensk diplomati och tidningspress under Krimkriget* (*Swedish diplomacy and newspapers during the Crimean War*), 1939, as well as by Allan Jansson, *Försvarsfrågan i svensk politik, från 1809 till Krimkriget* (*The defence question in Swedish politics from 1809 to the Crimean War*), 1935. Of all the Swedish writers, Eriksson is the clearest in his view that the King from September 1853 to December 1855 pursued a conscious line aiming at an alliance with Western Powers.[xxxvi] However, if Baumgart portrays Sweden as reacting to Allied actions, Eriksson seems to move somewhat too far in the other direction, with King Oscar, as it were, setting the entire agenda for the negotiations in 1855. This thesis will attempt to show that once the disappointing Baltic Campaign of 1854 was over, Swedish participation in the Crimean War could not realistically take place before the end of the Crimean Campaign, since the Allies could not fight a two-front land war.

C F Palmstierna in his published PhD thesis *Sverige, Ryssland och England 1833-1855 – Kring novembertraktatens förutsättningar, (Sweden, Russia and England 1833-1855, On the basis for the November Treaty)* takes a similar view to Eriksson. Palmstierna notes that Sweden's move from a Russian to a Western orbit was a decades-long process, rather than one of intermittent unusual events.[xxxvii] Palmstierna also points out that, following the Treaty of Unkiar-Skelessi in 1833, Britain began to look to the Baltic, where Russia was building a strong navy. Thenceforth, there were regular warnings in English press about Russia's ambition in the north and about Sweden's dependence on its neighbour.[xxxviii] The Swedish-Danish Neutrality Declaration and the negotiations leading up to the November Treaty are also covered in detail by Carl Michael Runeberg, in his published PhD thesis *Sveriges politik under Krimkriget, Neutralitetsförklaringen 1853-1854*, (*Swedish policy during the Crimean War, the Declaration of Neutrality 1853-1854*) and then in *Finland under Orientaliska Kriget* (*Finland during the Oriental War*). Together with Eriksson and Palmstierna, Runeberg has by far the most detailed description of the Swedish-Allied negotiations. However, where Eriksson has the King consciously and actively working towards an alliance with the Western Powers and Swedish participation in the war, Runeberg is less certain and notes that, without guarantees, King Oscar dared not break with his powerful neighbour.[xxxix]

It may seem puzzling that most of these Swedish-language sources date from before World War II. This has to do with a peculiar development in the Swedish attitude to history. The Social Democrats, who ruled Sweden from 1932 to 1976, were not particularly interested in promoting knowledge of Swedish history. If Swedes believed that there was a dismal and dreary past which ended in 1932, when the Social Democrats came to power and introduced the welfare state which made Sweden rich, then so much better. In consequence, very little Swedish history was actually written after World War II up to the mid-1980s. While there has since then been considerable interest in history, notably with biographies of historical persons regularly appearing, there is still a dearth of historical material compared with, eg, the UK or the United States. However, a recently published and excellent biography of King Oscar I by Eva Helen Ulvros (*Oscar I – en biografi*; *Oscar I – a biography*) briefly covers the Swedish involvement in the Crimean War, again making it clear that the King did want Sweden to take part in the war.[xl] Herman Lindqvist also touches briefly on it in his multi-volume *History of Sweden*, making the same point about King Oscar's aims. But

Lindqvist also has to be read with care since he has been found to be sloppy with facts in other parts of his work.[xli]

A further point needs to be made. Much of what has been written on the Swedish side concentrates on the King. Given that Sweden had a parliament (the Riksdag) and a government, which at least in theory, was answerable to parliament, why was this the case? The answer is that the King very much determined Swedish foreign policy and ran it as his private fief. Runeberg notes that the King would communicate directly with Swedish emissaries abroad or with foreign emissaries in Sweden, bypassing his government.[xlii] In consequence, Swedish cabinet minutes tend to be sparse and rarely concern foreign affairs. Eriksson shows how the Ministers of State for Foreign Affairs were kept in ignorance by the King (and if they happened to know more than they thought the King would appreciate, made sure he did not know how much they knew).[xliii] Runeberg shows that foreign emissaries were well aware of this; rather than referring to, eg, 'the Royal Government' or 'His Swedish Majesty's Government', their dispatches talk of 'the King of Sweden' or 'King Oscar'. Hence, any analysis of Swedish foreign policy at this time needs to concentrate on the King, although the actions of his ministers may still be of importance.

For most English-language historians, the Baltic Theatre was a sideshow in the Crimean War. This affects the amount of space they devote to it, as well as their general ignorance (with honourable exceptions!) of details surrounding the negotiations between Sweden and the Allies. It does not excuse the surprising amount of factual errors, even in books that devote greater space to the Baltic. By contrast, for Swedish-language historians, the Baltic Theatre and the discussions about a Swedish participation in the war, are the central theme. The difference between the two groups is perhaps greatest when it comes to the position of King Oscar I. English-language authors vary in their view on the King's aims, but – Baumgart excepted – tend to lean towards Royle's view that the King was opposed to joining the war and that his negotiating tactics were directed towards this aim.[xliv] By contrast, the divide between Swedish authors is between those – eg, Eriksson and Palmstierna – who feel that the King from the start wanted Sweden to take part in the war; and those – eg, Cullberg – who feel that he only shifted towards this stance as the conflict progressed (and the Emperor Nicholas I died).

This thesis aims to show that the negotiations between the Allies and Sweden were seriously intended on both sides. The Allies wanted Sweden to join the war and Sweden – or rather, King Oscar – wanted to join. It also contends that while Sweden's army, beyond its numbers, would have been of little use to the Allies, the Swedish navy could have made a more substantial contribution. But even without joining the war, Sweden, through the November Treaty, played a role in hastening its end. As to the last research question – why Sweden never joined the war – there are a number of answers. One is the outbreak of peace in 1856. But there are other reasons. The Allies lacked the capacity to fight a two-front land war. Once the focus of the war had shifted to the Crimea, they would not be able to fulfil Sweden's conditions for joining the war in terms of military assistance until the Crimean campaign was over. They could also hope that once this had happened, Russia would agree to peace. In addition, the Allies could never deliver Austrian participation in the war (another Swedish condition). Nor could they guarantee Swedish recovery of Finland (a third Swedish condition) or – crucially – that they would help Sweden retain this province for the future. On the Swedish side, the disappointing Allied performance in the 1854 Baltic Campaign was not calculated to raise any enthusiasm for taking part in the war. But a more fundamental answer seems to be that the keenness of the Allies in having Sweden join the war, never peaked at the same time as Sweden's interest in taking part.

Chapter 1

Setting the stage
The Crimean War

This chapter discusses the background to the Crimean War and gives an overview of military developments in the Crimea once the war had broken out. It attempts to examine whether the main cause of the war was the Eastern Question, with all its political and religious ramifications; or whether the war had more to do with the balance of power in Europe and British (notably) attempts to halt the rise of Russia. The chapter will argue that, while the dispute over the Holy Places was the trigger and the cause that made this particular war unavoidable, concerns about the balance of power in Europe were equally important for Britain and – to a lesser extent – for France. It is this that makes the Baltic Theatre more important than it would have been had the war solely concerned the Eastern Question.

The chapter also reviews the history of Swedish-Russian interaction in the Baltic until the mid-19th Century, including showing the balance of military power in the area at the outbreak of the Crimean War. This overview is necessary in order to explain King Oscar's actions. It shows that Sweden for most of the early 19th Century was perceived – both by Russia and by other countries – as a Russian satellite. By the middle of the century, Sweden was attempting to move away from the Russian orbit. The country was too weak to do this on its own. But in connection with a war, where Russia was tied up elsewhere, a diplomatic shift became possible. It was this long-term objective and the possibilities opened by the Crimean War that dictated much of Swedish thinking and acting.

By the mid-19th Century, the Ottoman Empire was still a powerful country, but one unmistakably in decline. The most aggressive of its neighbours, Russia, had gradually encroached on the Empire, eventually conquering the entire north coast of the Black Sea. Other European powers had nibbled at the Empire's edges – Austria in the Balkans, France in North Africa – while Serbs, Greeks and Mehmet Ali in Egypt were only the first subjects to carve out independent or quasi-independent states of their own. This gave ample opportunities for further meddling by the Empire's neighbours. In 1833, Russia intervened to support the Sultan against Mehmet Ali and was rewarded with the Treaty of Unkiar-Skelessi. Ostensibly a defensive treaty, a secret clause absolved Turkey from assisting Russia militarily, but instead obliged it to close the Straits – the Dardanelles and the Bosporus – to foreign warships.[xlv] Following this Treaty, Britain began to be more concerned about the safety of the route to India and henceforth the integrity of the Ottoman Empire became a vital interest for the British government.[xlvi] There were also repercussions in the North. English and French protests against the Treaty led to fears of war in Europe. King Karl XIV Johan of Sweden and Norway was worried lest the Scandinavian monarchy be dragged into such a conflict and issued the first proclamation of Swedish neutrality.[xlvii] The closing of the Black Sea to Britain also turned British eyes towards the Baltic, with regular warnings in British press about Russian ambitions in the North and about Sweden's dependence on its large neighbour.[xlviii]

Following a further war between the Sultan and Mehmet Ali, the Treaty of Unkiar-Skelessi was replaced in 1841 by the London Straits Convention, which banned foreign warships from entering the Straits, except those of Turkish allies in wartime. This shifted Russian policy from continuous encroachment on the Ottoman Empire to one of maintaining its integrity as a barrier to keep other powers from entering the Straits. Should Turkey collapse, Russia intended that the fate of its territory was to be negotiated with the other powers.[xlix]

This was the line pursued by Emperor Nicholas I of Russia when he visited Britain in 1844. While the British government did not wish to enter into any binding commitment, Nicholas I came away from his visit with a clear impression that Russian and British interests were aligned.[l] Although the British government eventually began to doubt the Russian Emperor's good intention, he remained convinced of the fundamental commonality of British and Russian interests.[li]

After the European revolutions of 1848 and – notably – the establishment in France of the Second Republic, the situation changed; and changed again when the President of the Republic, Prince Louis Napoleon, seized power and transformed himself into Emperor Napoleon III. The new Emperor was keen on obtaining the support of the Catholic Church in France. Already before the *coup d'état* that re-established the Empire, the French Ambassador to the Porte, had demanded that Turkey honour the Treaty of 1740 which had granted France 'sovereign rights' in the Holy Land.[lii] On 9th February 1852, the Porte agreed the validity of the Latin claims. However, the French efforts led to Russian counter-efforts and a *firman* (decree) confirmed the rights of the Orthodox Church and in the process revoked those just confirmed to the French.[liii] Over the course of the next 16 months, French and Russian pressure on the Porte led to alternating decisions, with the British ambassador generally mediating, supporting Turkey against Russia but also counselling the Turks to at the same time announce and implement domestic reforms, ameliorating the situation of the Christians.

Ultimately – and after a show of force – the French claims prevailed. In December 1852, the Latin clergy were given one of the keys to the Church of the Nativity in Bethlehem and permission to affix a silver star, emblazoned with the arms of France, in the Crypt of the Manger.[liv]

This was unacceptable to the Russian Emperor, who now embarked on a two-pronged strategy aimed at reversing the Latin gains and at least entrenching Russian domination over the Ottoman Empire, at most aiming at dismembering that realm.[lv] The former would already be achieved by reasserting Russia's position as protector over and intercessor for the Orthodox Christians ruled by the Sultan. Muslims probably were a narrow majority of the 24 million or so Ottoman subjects. But, in Europe, the 11-12 million Orthodox Christians far outnumbered the 2 million Muslims. By becoming their guardian power, Russia would by default come to dominate at least the European part of the Ottoman Empire – including the capital Constantinople. In order to achieve his aims, Nicholas I in February 1853 sent a diplomatic mission headed by Prince A S Menshikov to Constantinople.

For the second object – the possible dismemberment of the Ottoman Empire, the Russian Emperor initially turned to Britain for support. Over the course of January and February 1853, the Emperor approached the British Ambassador to St Petersburg, Sir Hamilton Seymour. During the course of these 'Seymour Conversations', the Emperor outlined a proposed partition plan. The exact nature of this plan varied slightly over time. But regardless of the details, the British government did not take the bait, only disclaiming any desire for Constantinople and noting that so too did Russia.[lvi]

Nor was Prince Menshikov's mission successful – at least not if the aim was to reverse the Latin gains. But it is not clear that this was ever the ultimate intention. According to Curtiss, the Russian Emperor had as early as late 1852 decided on war with Turkey.[lvii] The use of Prince Menshikov to head the mission implied as much. Kinglake claims that Menshikov was picked specifically because he would not moderate the Emperor's demands and his feelings and prejudices were likely to cause him to embitter the dispute.[lviii] By contrast, Eriksson asserts that Russia did not want war, but that Menshikov's clumsiness and vague instructions nevertheless brought about that result.[lix] However, a few factors argue against this view. First, the Russian demands, notably for recognition of Russia' protective rights over Turkey's Orthodox subjects were difficult, if not impossible for Turkey to accept.[lx] Second, the Menshikov mission was accompanied by advanced plans for a military strike against Constantinople.[lxi] Third, Menshikov's character, as noted above, made him eminently unsuitable for a peace-seeking mission. General Gustaf de Nordin, the Swedish Minister to St Petersburg, reports Menshikov loudly declaring in Odessa that he was "going to Constantinople to teach the Sultan to eat pork"; and later writing back from Constantinople that he "was at the moment busy mounting a restless horse named Sultan but that he would eventually succeed perfectly well in taming him and making him docile".[lxii]

In any case, the Menshikov mission ultimately failed. Shortly afterwards, Russia issued an ultimatum to Turkey, which, upon its rejections was followed on 2nd July 1853 by Russian occupation of the Danube Principalities. This did not immediately mean war. The Russian occupation was presented as a means to exert pressure on Turkey to accept the Russian demands. In spite of continued diplomacy, this was unsuccessful and on 4th October 1853, Turkey declared war on Russia. On 22nd October, an Anglo-French fleet entered the Dardanelles and on 29th October an Ottoman army crossed into Wallachia. The actual course of the war in the Black Sea region is only tangentially of importance to this thesis and will only be covered cursorily.

On 4th November, the Ottoman General Omar Pasha defeated the Russians in the Battle of Oltenitza. On 25th November, Britain and France signed a defensive alliance with Turkey. Five days later, a Russian squadron destroyed a Turkish naval detachment in Sinope. Although the two powers were already at war, this was presented in Western Europe as 'The Massacre of Sinope', the more appalling because of the presence of an Allied fleet in the Dardanelles, and greatly added to the popular pressure for war against Russia. On 8th January 1854 the Allied fleet sailed into the Bosporus and on 27th February an Anglo-French ultimatum demanded that Russia evacuate the Danubian Principalities. On 27th March 1854, France declared war on Russia, followed one day later by Great Britain.

Initially, the Allied expeditionary force was sent to Varna on the European Black Sea coast. However, the Turkish army turned out not to need much help. In early September, the Allied troops were instead shifted to the Crimea with a view to destroying the large Russian naval base at Sevastopol. At the Battle of Alma on 19th September 1854, a Russian attempt to stop the Allied march on Sevastopol was defeated, and the city was besieged from 8th October. The Russians made two major attempts to break the siege, in the battles of Balaklava (25th October 1854) and Inkerman (5th November 1854), both of which were defeated. Two further unsuccessful attempts were made in 1855 (Eupatoria on 15th February and Traktir Ridge on 16th August). Meanwhile, Allied attempts to storm the defences of Sevastopol were finally successful in September 1855 and on the 9th of that month the Russians evacuated the city, with the Allies marching in on the 12th. This effectively brought military operations in the Crimea to an end.

Throughout the conflict, diplomatic negotiations had continued between the belligerent parties, with Austria playing a key role as an intermediary. From August 1854 onwards, the Allied demands, supported by Austria, centred on the so-called Four Points. These were:

The Russian protectorate over the Danube Principalities to be replaced by a European guarantee;

Navigation on the Danube to be free;

The Straits Convention of 1841 to be revised in the interests of the Balance of Power in Europe;

Russia to renounce its claims to a protectorate over the Orthodox, to be replaced by a Turkish guarantee for all Christians to the five powers.[lxiii]

The Third Point was eventually replaced by a demand for the Russian naval presence in the Black Sea to be limited. Finally, a Fifth Point was added, giving the Allies the right to raise any further issues they considered necessary.[lxiv] The latter two issues both have a bearing on the Swedish and Baltic questions, as will be shown below. Following further negotiations in the autumn of 1855 and finally an Austro-Allied ultimatum, Russia accepted the Five Points on 15th January 1856. Peace was signed in Paris on 30th March 1856.

Why did the Crimean War break out? This issue already exercised contemporaries. Could it really be that modern European countries went to war (in Lord Clarendon's, the British Foreign Secretary's, words) "on account of a doorkey, a silverstar and the mending of a dilapidated dome"?[lxv] The question of 'why' is very much connected with 'for what', the aims of the different belligerent powers. However, for the purposes of this thesis, they key issues are the French and British motivations, as these are important for developments in the Baltic.

French reasons for going to war were complicated. In one sense, France went to war to protect the gains of the Latin Church in the Holy Land, just as it had at least threatened the Ottoman Empire with war in order to achieve these gains. These French efforts on behalf of the Catholics in the Middle East were due to the fragility of the new French regime.[lxvi] But France had wider aims as well. The President – from December 1852, the Emperor Napoleon III – aimed at revising the entire European order of 1815 and restore France to its role as a first-rank European power. He also had wide-ranging, if subsidiary aims, including if possible restoring an independent Poland and altering the balance of power in the Italian Peninsula in favour of Sardinia.[lxvii] Kinglake lays all the blame for the war on the French President and claims that the war was thought up by him as an attempt to distract attention from his seizure of power and his rule.[lxviii] This seems to be an exaggerated view. By contrast, in *The Life and Letters of George William Frederick Fourth Earl of Clarendon,* Sir Herbert Maxwell claims that Napoleon III was a frank and loyal ally throughout the war.[lxix]

For Britain, the reasons for war seem to have been a mixture. Baumgart lists concerns about the route to India – noting that the route via Egypt had begun to become more important than the longer voyage around the Cape of Good Hope – as well as commercial interests and the aim of preserving the integrity of the Ottoman Empire.[lxx] But he also points out that both France and Britain proclaimed that they were fighting to uphold the European balance of power – as will be seen, a key concern in the negotiations with Sweden.[lxxi] Curtiss agrees that the war also was about stopping the expansion of Russian power, not only in the Levant but elsewhere.[lxxii]

Swedish attitudes will be covered extensively in later chapters. However, there is one more country, namely Austria, whose aims need to be touched upon. Initially and for much of the war, the King of Sweden explicitly tied his countries' participation in the war to Austria joining as well. However, Baumgart shows that Austria was unlikely to take an active part in the war. Austria was the quintessential *status quo* power.[lxxiii] It was frightened of Russian expansion and saw the Ottoman Empire as a bulwark against Russian encroachment in the Balkans.[lxxiv] Moreover, the Russian advance into the Balkans encouraged revolutionary tendencies among the Ottoman subject peoples there, something that threatened to spill over into the Austrian dominions. This pushed Austria closer to the Western Powers.[lxxv] However, the Austrian Foreign Minister Count Buol von Schauenstein also feared that the longer the war lasted, the greater the pressure on Austria to take part; while going to war against Russia would eventually leave Austria to face Russia's wrath alone.[lxxvi] The latter – being left alone to face a vengeful Russia – was also a concern for the Swedish King. Austria's aims ultimately boiled down to forcing a Russian evacuation of the Danubian Principalities, followed by their Austrian occupation. This was achieved as early as August 1854. Thenceforth, Austria's main role was as a mediator between Russia and the Allies, albeit a mediator with more than one foot in the Allied camp. Austria repeatedly implied to the Allies that it was ready to join them if Russia rejected their demands. However, some historians – eg, Curtiss and Runeberg – believe that Austria played a double game throughout the war, with the aim of avoiding having to take part.[lxxvii] Hence, by tying Swedish participation in the war to Austria, King Oscar let himself be guided by the most uncertain and hesitant of all the European powers.[lxxviii]

The Crimean War – like all wars – had a number of causes. Some were regional – the issue of the Holy Places and the Christians in the Ottoman Empire and the fate of the Empire itself. Others were more general – the desire to limit Russian expansion or the aim to revise the balance of power in Europe. Which of these aims dominated the war aims at any one stage played a key role in determining the course of the negotiations in the Baltic.

The Baltic until 1852

Warfare between Sweden and Russia goes back centuries. Although the fortunes of war were mixed, Sweden initially advanced at Russia's expense, reaching its territorial peak in the East with the Treaty of Stolbova in 1617. Thenceforth, Swedish fortune generally waned. From the Great Northern War (1700-1721) to the Finnish War (1808-1809), Sweden gradually lost all its trans-Baltic territories, culminating with the loss of Finland, as well as parts of the Swedish provinces of Västerbotten and Lappland in the north and the Swedish Åland Islands in the mid-Baltic.

The Finnish War led to a *coup d'état* in Sweden. King Gustav IV Adolf was deposed and replaced by his uncle, King Karl XIII. However, the latter was childless and thus only a stopgap solution. Eventually, one of Napoleon's Marshals, Jean Baptiste Bernadotte, was elected Crown Prince and adopted by the King. The main reason for choosing a Marshal of France was the hope that he would restore Sweden's military fortunes, specifically by recovering Finland from Russia.

These hopes were swiftly disappointed. Bernadotte became Crown Prince of Sweden in 1810. The King was already old (61) and tired (possibly senile) and the Crown Prince quickly became the *de facto* ruler of the realm. However, instead of joining Napoleon in his attack on Russia, the new ruler saw his – and perhaps his country's – best interest in an alliance with the hereditary enemy and opposition to France. At the time of Bernadotte's election, Sweden was nominally at war with Britain, having been forced to join the Continental System in late 1810. For the time being, this war had seen no fighting, but French pressure on Sweden to play a more active role kept increasing, culminating in French occupation of Swedish Pomerania in January 1812. At an extraordinary meeting of the Swedish cabinet on 21st and 24th February 1812, it was decided that Sweden would make peace with Britain, if necessary break with France and secretly approach Russia. The ostensible aim of this policy was to "achieve complete neutrality".[lxxix] In April the same year Sweden concluded a treaty with Russia, where the two countries recognised each other's possessions – in other words, Sweden recognised that Finland was permanently lost – and Russia promised an army to help Sweden conquer Norway. (This was not realised due to the French invasion of Russia.) In August 1812, Bernadotte (henceforth referred to as Karl Johan while Crown Prince and Karl XIV Johan when King) met Emperor Alexander I in Åbo, the capital of Finland. Eventually, Sweden joined the alliance against Napoleon and was rewarded with Norway.

Karl Johan's motives for this policy – later dubbed 'the policy of 1812' – were multifaceted. He had no emotional attachment to Finland, but a clear eye for the advantage he and Sweden could gain from detaching Norway from Denmark and incorporating it with Sweden. Moreover, by 1812 he assumed that France was losing the Napoleonic wars. Even if Sweden managed to reconquer Finland, it would be unable to withstand Russian attempts to retake the province – even less so if Russia was backed by the other European powers. Karl Johan may also have aimed at becoming Emperor or King of France – something that could only be achieved with the help of the anti-French coalition. Finally, his position in Sweden was not wholly secure; Finland, if reconquered, would be part of Sweden. By contrast Norway became a separate kingdom in personal union with Sweden – a potential bolthole in case Karl Johan was toppled from his Swedish throne.

The changed Swedish policy safeguarded Karl Johan's throne. It stabilised Sweden's foreign relations – but led to Russian dominance of Sweden. The policy also led to British suspicion of Sweden, something that may have influenced the British side in the Crimean War negotiations.[lxxx] To shake off this Russian 'wardship' became a Swedish goal throughout the first half of the 19th Century.[lxxxi]

In spite of Sweden's Russian-oriented policy, a substantial amount of hostility to Russia remained. The public debate generally assumed a rivalry between Russia and Britain, with Liberals generally claiming that Sweden was closer to Britain. Even with a pro-Russian foreign policy, Sweden's defence policy saw Britain as a natural ally and Russia as a natural enemy.[lxxxii] Admiral Count Baltzar von Platen, a member of the Swedish government and at one stage Lord Lieutenant of Norway, put it plainly to Karl Johan: "Je ne reconnois a la Scandinavie qu'un alliée naturel: l'Angleterre; un ennemi naturel: la Russie" ("For Scandinavia I only recognise one natural ally: England, and one natural enemy: Russia").[lxxxiii] This also affected the development of the Swedish armed forces. The magazine *Allmänna Journalen* wrote on 17th February 1829; "Out of ten wars that the Scandinavian Peninsula henceforth is likely to wage, it can probably safely be said that England in 7 or 8 will be its ally, for this reason, that it must always be in the English interest to have a fixed support in Scandinavia for the sake of its important and large trade in the Baltic."[lxxxiv] This meant that the Scandinavian kingdoms needed to have armed forces that could defend them as well as complement its putative ally's likely expeditionary force. Proponents of a pro-British policy argued in favour of building a brown-water (ie, archipelagic) navy, suited to operations in the Baltic, as opposed to a blue-water (high seas) fleet. Of course, the argument also worked in reverse – proponents of a brown-water navy needed to hold out the prospect of a British alliance in wartime, as the Royal Navy would be needed to complement the Swedish armed forces.[lxxxv]

This strange dichotomy between a pro-Russian foreign policy and an anti-Russian popular feeling and defence policy continued throughout the first half of the 19th Century. However, until the Crimean War, it was not put to the test. The closest occasion came in 1834, when French and British protests against the Treaty of Unkiar-Skelessi briefly threatened war between these countries and Russia. At this stage, Karl XIV Johan issued Sweden's first declaration of neutrality. Contrary to 1853 this was seen as a pro-Russian gesture. That was partly due to events surrounding the declaration. The Swedish and Danish governments had discussed a joint declaration of neutrality, but this was blocked by Russian intervention.[lxxxvi] For Russia, this confirmed Sweden's position as a semi-vassal. The fact that British ships could use Swedish ports remained an irritant, but, broadly speaking, Sweden remained pro-Russian. Moreover, by blocking Swedish-Danish cooperation, an incipient Scandinavist[lxxxvii] policy was (perhaps unintentionally) nipped in the bud.[lxxxviii] But this also raised the profile of the Baltic in Britain. The British Minister to Stockholm, Lord Howard de Walden, had tried in 1833 to change Sweden's policy in a more pro-British direction, supported in his endeavours by the then Foreign Secretary Lord Palmerston.[lxxxix] Moreover, from this time onwards, there were regular warnings in British press about Russia's ambitions in the north and about Sweden's dependence on its neighbour.[xc] This was also the tenor of a longer report to Palmerston in 1836 by John Rice Crowe, at that stage British Vice-Consul in Hammerfest in Norway and later Consul in Kristiania (Oslo). Crowe's report outlined the history of northern Scandinavia and in particular putative Russian designs on an ice-free port on the northern coast of Norway – from which, Crowe pointed out, a Russian force could descend on Scotland in a matter of days.[xci] This report would return to play a part in the build-up to the November Treaty.

In the Oriental Crisis of 1840-1841, Sweden once again found itself on the same side as Russia – but so too did Britain. Significantly, Sweden again attempted to work with Denmark to achieve a common neutrality.[xcii]

On its own, however, Sweden had a problem. Its armed forces, while large, were weak. Throughout the 19th Century, Swedish politics were dominated by a number of major issues, one of which was defence reform.

The core of the Swedish army was still based on the Indelningsverk (the term is generally used without translation). The system, similar to the Prussian cantonment, relied on soldiers receiving farms (according to rank) and tenants equipping and supplying soldiers instead of paying rent. This enabled a large army in relation to the size of the population. A comparison in *Göteborgs Handels- och Sjöfarts Tidning* on 4th January 1854, showed that Sweden had 15 indelta (mobilised through the indelningsverk) soldiers per 100 inhabitants, compared with 10 in France, somewhat less than 10 in Sardinia and somewhat more than 10 in The Netherlands. At this stage, Sweden's armed forces comprised some 144,000 men, of which 7,000 salaried (ie, full-time), 33,400 indelta and 95,200 beväringar (recruits), a category introduced in 1812. But the quality of the latter – intended as reserves and replacement for the indelta soldiers – was doubtful. They exercised for less than two weeks per annum, during which they fired three rounds of ammunition.[xciii]

Although the weakness of the army was apparent to observers, reform was complicated by the fact that the Indelningsverk meant that defence issues were tightly involved with issues of privileges and taxation.[xciv]

Moreover, Sweden's army was always going to be smaller than its Russian foes. The Swedish defence debate generally seems to have underestimated the size of the Russian army. In 1830, it was assumed that Russia could deploy some 30-40,000 men against Sweden, ie, not much more than the core Swedish army. By 1861 – after the Crimean War – the number was assumed to be 100,000, but for logistical reasons, only 35,000 of these could be shipped across the Baltic.[xcv] However, the Russian armed forces at the beginning of the Crimean War totalled between 900,000 and 1 million men plus Cossacks.[xcvi] While many of these were used for garrison duty around the vast Empire, the forces in Finland, the Baltic Provinces and around St Petersburg during the Crimean War totalled between 250,000 and 300,000 men, far outnumbering the Swedish forces.[xcvii]

The Swedish navy had also been left to decay. At the outbreak of the war, the Swedish navy could muster five or six ships of the line (of which four in various stages of repair), five frigates plus one more being built, some smaller sailing ships and some 200 gunboats of different calibres.[xcviii] Around the same time, the Norwegian navy consisted of four frigates and another 129 gunboats.[xcix] In 1843, a joint defence committee from both kingdoms planned for a fleet equal in size to the Russian Baltic Fleet.[c] But this would necessitate a 40% rise in the naval estimates, something at least the Swedish

Riksdag was bound to vote down.[ci] In the Swedish debate, it was assumed that the Russian Baltic Fleet would consist of 30-40 capital ships; a navy able to match this would have cost more than the entire Swedish armed forces.[cii] In addition to the size, here too there was an issue of quality. The last cruise of a Swedish ship of the line prior to the Crimean War took place in 1836.[ciii] By contrast, the Emperor Nicholas I had spent much time and effort on strengthening the Russian Baltic Fleet – to the considerable concern of British successive Ministers to St Petersburg.[civ] By the outbreak of the war, the Russian Baltic Fleet consisted of 24 ships of the line and 7 frigates, none of which were steamships, 23 armed steamers and a number of gunboats, based in Kronstadt and Sveaborg, with smaller detachments of gunboats elsewhere.[cv]

Sweden was thus outnumbered, both on land and on sea. But the issue was never whether Sweden could take on the Russian Empire on its own. Rather, the question is whether the Swedish armed forces could contribute meaningfully to a joint effort with the Allies. Here Sweden did have one major asset – its 200 gunboats. The Baltic Sea, particularly the areas around the Russian bases Kronstadt, Sveaborg and Bomarsund, is not suitable for deep-going warships. But it is eminently suited for small gunboats. These are also likely to be more efficient against fortresses – a point raised repeatedly by Admiral Sir Charles Napier with the British Admiralty.[cvi] C I Hamilton claims that the Swedish gunboats, not being steam-driven, would not have been of much use.[cvii] But he also notes that the Admiralty from the start expected Sweden to join the war and so have the use of the Swedish gunboats.[cviii] Sweden might be outgunned and outnumbered – but to contemporaries, its gunboats were a major asset.

By the middle of the 19th Century Sweden was ripe for a change of foreign alignment. Anti-Russian feeling increased after the Polish Revolt in 1830, with considerable Swedish support for the rebels.[cix] The new King – Karl XIV Johan had died in 1844 and been succeeded by his son Oscar I – believed that Russia had to expand and expected a showdown between Russia and the Western Powers.[cx] His son, Crown Prince Karl, although a Conservative in contrast with his more Liberal father, also deeply hated Russia and everything Russian.[cxi]

As explained above (p. 10), Swedish foreign policy was very much decided by the King. Karl XIV Johan was firmly pro-Russian; his son Oscar I much less so. Cullberg claims that if the Emperor Nicholas I had not died, King Oscar would never have deviated from his policy of strict neutrality.[cxii] Royle also claims that Oscar was pro-Russian.[cxiii] But this is almost certainly a mistake. Eriksson throughout his book makes a reasoned argument that Oscar from the start intended Sweden to join the war against Russia. The King's disappointment at the Russian acceptance of the Four Points is amply attested by contemporary observers.[cxiv] More to the point, if the King never intended to deviate from his strict neutrality, there was no reason to maintain the extended negotiations with the Allies. It is true that there were concerns expressed in the defence debate that, a weak Swedish navy could tempt either Britain or Russia to seize the island of Gotland in the case of war.[cxv] But a British attack on Sweden in a war against Russia was always less likely. For one thing, it would add not just one, but most likely two enemies. Denmark was generally pro-Russian and – with memories of the Napoleonic Wars – above all anti-British. A British attack on Sweden would almost certainly have put Russian and Swedish pressure on Denmark to join them. The net result would have been to move the northern front – and the Russian navy – from the Baltic to the Sound, a narrow waterway and easy to close off; and 1,150 kilometres closer to British shores.

Moreover, the King's own writings make it clear that he feared Russian expansion, just as his common thread throughout the negotiations with the Allies was that the war aim of limiting Russia's expansion in Europe must be clearly stated.[cxvi] Hence, although Sweden was a Russian satellite, there were powerful forces in favour of escaping the Russian embrace.

However, for this to happen there had to be an alternative. The internal Swedish defence debate clearly identified this alternative as Great Britain. But was Britain interested? The

'Policy of 1812' generally made Britain suspicious of Swedish motives. But, at least from the 1840s, British politicians were concerned about potential Russian designs on northern Norway, where it was feared that the Empire aimed to build a large naval base in an ice-free port within easy reach of the British islands.[cxvii] In September 1851, Lord Palmerston, at that stage Foreign Secretary, wrote to Sir Edmund Lyons, the British Minister in Stockholm, urging him to dissuade the Swedish government from ceding any territory in Norway to Russia.[cxviii] By the time the Crimean War became imminent, British politicians and planners were already taking a possible Swedish alliance into account.[cxix] In August 1853, the Foreign Secretary Lord Clarendon wrote to Sir Edmund Lyons that "Sweden-Norway's true interests push it towards an alliance with England where it is seen in the friendliest way. – The character and habits and natural interests of the two countries render their Alliance both natural and desirable and I need not assure you that the earnest wish of Her Majesty's Govt is to promote it by every means in their power. You are instructed to make known these opinions in the quarters where you may consider they will produce a useful effect."[cxx] Admiral Sir Charles Napier's instructions for the 1854 Baltic Expedition included the protection of neutral territory from a Russian attack.[cxxi] In early March 1854 – ie, before war was declared – the British Foreign Secretary Lord Clarendon twice hinted at British support for Sweden to the Swedish Chargé d'Affaires in London, Baron de Geer.[cxxii] It is also clear that the British government hoped that Admiral Napier would obtain the services of Swedish (and Norwegian) sailors and pilots, something that would at least have been difficult if Sweden adhered to strict neutrality.[cxxiii]

By the middle of the 19th Century Sweden was ready to shift its political alignment. But doing so alone could prove difficult, as had been shown in 1834. Hence, Sweden needed outside assistance. The Crimean War meant that there were outside powers interested in facilitating such a shift. But in order to attract outside help, Sweden had to make the first move out of the Russian orbit.

Chapter 2: 1853: The Neutrality Declaration

This chapter covers the negotiations between Sweden and Denmark that culminated in a joint Declaration of Neutrality in December 1853; and the reactions of the warring powers to that Declaration. It argues that Swedish neutrality marked a shift away from the Russian orbit; and that Russia recognised this and showed its displeasure by treating Denmark and Sweden differently. The chapter further shows that although Sweden claimed to be strictly neutral, its neutrality was tilted in favour of the Allies, opening the possibility for a further shift into the anti-Russian camp.

Both in 1834 and in 1840/41, Sweden and Denmark had discussed a common policy of neutrality. In both cases, the cause of tension was in the Near East. In 1834 it was brought on by the Treaty of Unkiar-Skelessi and the threat of war between Russia on the one side and Britain and France on the other. In 1840/41 the threat of war was between France on the one side (supporting Mehmet Ali and Egypt) and Russia and Britain on the other. In 1834 discussions of a joint declaration of neutrality, although these were interrupted by Russian intervention.[cxxiv] Instead, Sweden unilaterally proclaimed its neutrality. Although generally perceived as pro-Russian, the Swedish policy still allowed British ships to use Swedish ports, and in this sense, was beneficial to Britain as well.[cxxv] The 1840/41 crisis never reached the stage of formal declarations of neutrality. However, by the time another Oriental Crisis appeared on the horizon in 1852/1853, it was already natural for the two Nordic Kingdoms to approach each other and discuss a common policy. So much so, in fact, that their respective approaches to each other coincided almost exactly in time. On 8th July 1853, Count Scheel-Plessen, Danish Minister to Stockholm, reported to his government that he had discreetly sounded out the Swedish government (most likely through Baron Ludvig Manderström, King Oscar's confidant) about its intentions.[cxxvi] The King's absence from his capital had meant that the Swedish reply beyond the aim of maintaining strict neutrality, had been "in a vague manner, but by no means evasive".[cxxvii] However, Scheel-Plessen felt it likely that the Swedish government eventually would contact the Danish government and referred in his dispatch to the negotiations of 1834 as a template for the discussions that he expected would ensue. One week later, on 15th July 1853, Baron Stierneld, the Swedish Prime Minister for Foreign Affairs, wrote to Baron af Wetterstedt, the Swedish Chargé d'Affaires in Copenhagen, enclosing a *Mémoire Confidentiel* to be delivered to the Danish Foreign Minister. This contained a formal invitation to Denmark, suggesting that the three Kingdoms (Denmark, Sweden and Norway) issue a joint and identical Declaration of Neutrality.[cxxviii] This Declaration was to be based on the principles of the 1834 Swedish Declaration, specifically:

No taking part in the imminent conflict;

Allowing the warships and trading ships of the warring parties to make use of the Kingdoms' ports, with the exception of certain military ports;

Selling goods to the warring parties, with the exception of contraband of war;

Freedom to trade with the warring parties, albeit with due attention to effective blockades; and

Not allowing prizes to be brought into the Kingdoms' ports (with the exception of ships in distress) and not to allow their sale in Sweden and Norway.[cxxix]

Although the Nordic Kingdoms were both interested in a common policy, they approached it with different aims. For King Oscar, one aim was to make Swedish neutrality more secure. If Sweden and Denmark issued joint and identical Declarations of Neutrality, it would be more difficult for Russia to demand changes in the Swedish policy. He also seems to have been motivated by Scandinavist feelings, hoping to succeed the childless Danish King Frederik VII and uniting the Nordic Kingdoms.[cxxx] For the Danish government, Swedish cooperation was welcome – but Denmark also wanted to involve the main German powers through its membership of the German Confederation by virtue of the personal union between Denmark and Schleswig-Holstein.[cxxxi] However, the Danish approaches were treated coldly by the German powers.[cxxxii] Sweden also approached the German powers, but in this case more to receive support for its definitions of neutrality, than to bring them into a wider neutrality convention.[cxxxiii]

One key issue for Sweden was the principle that a neutral flag should protect not only the ship, but also the cargo. Since the British government did not agree with this view, it could become a sticking point in getting the warring parties to respect the Nordic neutrality[cxxxiv]

The negotiations between Sweden and Denmark continued during the autumn of 1853. At this stage, both sides in the eventual conflict expressed an interest in Swedish neutrality. Lord Clarendon wrote to Sir Edmund Lyons on 12th September 1853 that "I hope we may not be involved in war, but if it should unfortunately take place I trust that Sweden will remain *strictly* neutral, and more than that we have no right to demand, but less we should not be disposed to accept."[cxxxv] On the Russian side, already as early as 28th July 1853, General de Nordin, the Swedish Minister to St Petersburg, had a meeting with the Russian Foreign Minister Count Nesselrode, where the latter told him "If war breaks out, I suppose that you would remain perfectly neutral, and that is all that we would wish and that we would demand of you in that case; but you can safely report to your Court that a break between England and us on account of the Oriental Question is hardly to fear."[cxxxvi]

On 28th October 1853, Count Sparre, Swedish Prime Minister for Justice and acting Prime Minister for Foreign Affairs, sent a detailed proposal for a Neutrality Declaration to Minister Lagerheim in Copenhagen. This generally agreed with the proposal of 14th July, but with two changes. The first referred to the naval ports: The United Kingdoms would not close their naval ports to warships of the combatants but would close some of the inner harbours in such ports and also in detail regulate warship visits to naval ports. The second point was a refusal to recognise letters of marque and to refuse all access to privateers. After some discussion, the Danish government agreed in principle to the Swedish proposals.

The initial plan had been for Sweden and Denmark to issue their Declarations of Neutrality at the same time. King Oscar had also hoped that the negotiations would be confidential and not lead to any questions from the great powers. However, this foundered, partly because of the different leanings of the two courts. Denmark was historically more pro-Russian than Sweden (not least in order to balance Sweden) and, because of its involvement in German affairs, more concerned about the reactions of the German states. Sweden's main interest was to achieve acceptance of its neutrality from the warring states. In October 1853, Baron Plessen, the Danish Minister to St Petersburg, brought up the issue of Denmark's intended neutrality with the Russian government.[cxxxvii] More worryingly from a Swedish perspective, Plessen's comments implied that Denmark in some situations could need Russian help, eg, if the Royal Navy tried to winter in Denmark in order to prepare for an early entry into the Baltic. Following Plessen's conversation with Nesselrode, the Russian Chancellor wrote a dispatch to the Russian Minister in Stockholm, Jacob Andreyevich Dashkov, with instructions to pass it on to the Swedish government. While making it clear that the Imperial government was not attempting to press the Swedish government for a statement of its attitude in a possible war, the dispatch nevertheless implied that Sweden would take a pro-Russian attitude – specifically, that the ports of the United Kingdoms would be closed to warships from countries at war with Russia.[cxxxviii] In consequence, the Swedish government felt less constrained to act jointly with Denmark and on 7th November 1853, Count Piper from the Swedish legation in St Petersburg read out a note about Sweden's likely neutrality to Nesselrode. The latter's reaction was positive but again clearly implied that Russia expected Sweden's neutrality to be pro-Russian ("nous souhaitons, nous attendons de l'amitié que porte le Roi à Notre Souverain, que cette neutralité nous soit tou-à-fait bienveillant" – "we wish, we expect from the friendship that the King bears our Sovereign, that this neutrality will be wholly benevolent to us").[cxxxix] In fact, de Nordin had already in June written to Manderström, indicating that Russia's preference probably was for the Baltic to be completely closed to all navies. However, de Nordin also noted that even combined, the Swedish, Danish and Russian navies would be incapable of achieving this aim.[cxl]

Following further negotiations between the two Nordic courts, the Danish government accepted the slightly amended Swedish proposal on 10th November.

Declaring neutrality was one thing; getting it accepted by the potentially warring parties, was another. On 20th December 1853, the two governments issued their joint Declaration of Neutrality. On 2nd January 1854, they were delivered to the British and French foreign secretaries. The initial reaction from both countries was positive (eg, Lord Clarendon's comment after he had read the notes, "Well, it appears really to be a strict neutrality."[cxli]). However, neither country initially committed itself to an unqualified acceptance.

With reference to British acceptance, the main hurdle was the Swedish attitude that the neutral flag should protect both the ship and the cargo. This was not only a sticking point between Britain and the Scandinavian Kingdoms; France and the United States shared the Scandinavian view. In the end, the French view was crucial in persuading the British government to approve the Swedish neutrality.[cxlii] In fact, Jonasson claims that the changing British attitude towards the rights of neutrals is one of the lasting effects of the Crimean War.[cxliii]

Getting Russian approval proved more complicated. When Count Piper had informed Nesselrode of the intended Swedish neutrality, the Russian Foreign Minister had suggested that Sweden should close its ports to powers at war with Russia. Although the news that among the ports closed would be Slite on the Baltic island of Gotland, the nearest Swedish port to Russia was welcomed by Nesselrode (when Piper read out the names of closed ports, the Chancellor interrupted him when Slite was mentioned, exclaiming "Ah, ceci est très important, ce port étant si près de nous" – "Ah, this is very important, this port being so close to us"[cxliv]), the Russian government still felt that Sweden's neutrality was insufficiently pro-Russian. Consequently, it initially refused to recognise Sweden's neutrality. However, Denmark's neutrality was immediately accepted, with reference to its different geographical position. The Russian objections were transmitted directly to the King through Dashkov. In reply, King Oscar noted that it would be impossible for Sweden to successfully defend its long coastline against a fleet determined to gain entry to a port, so that closing all ports to foreign warships would be to issue a decree that he lacked the power to enforce. Moreover, by closing the port of Slite, the most important Baltic port, and by strongly fortifying Gotland, he had clearly acted in Russia's interests. Finally, the King expressed his anger that the Danish Declaration of Neutrality had been treated differently from the Swedish.[cxlv]

The Swedish government's formal reply rejected the Russian demands. Moreover, King Oscar wrote a personal letter to the Russian Emperor explaining his and his country's actions. As a result, Nesselrode told Piper that Russia would abandon its demands for a modification of Sweden's neutrality.[cxlvi] However, this did not mean immediate recognition of Sweden's neutrality. Both Nesselrode and the Russian Emperor wrote further letters to the Swedish government and King. Nesselrode's letter expressed the hope that the friendly feelings of King Oscar and his government towards Russia would not change. The Emperor's letter was more personal, mentioning the friendship between the two rulers' fathers (Karl XIV Johan and Alexander I) as well as their own friendship which had been tested as recently as 1848. Referring to this, the Emperor wrote "It is this which allows me to think that, in the new struggle that may perhaps break out, the arms of Your Majesty, solely aimed at respecting His neutrality, will in no case be turned against Russia. I dare hope that He will not refuse to give me a positive assurance of this, like Your August Father did not hesitate to give to the Emperor Alexander. His word will satisfy me as I have full faith in it, and it is in this way that I ask Your Majesty to agree to such an assurance etc"[cxlvii] In many ways, what Russia here seemed to have aimed at was a re-establishment of the treaty and policy of 1812. If so, it failed. The King's reply was polite, but firmly rejected the Emperor's request, claiming that the kind of assurance asked would be the same as an alliance and so be seen as incompatible with neutrality by other powers; and that he could only abandon his neutrality by turning against powers that attempted to force him to do so.[cxlviii] As a result, Russia finally recognised the Swedish neutrality on 7th March 1854 – although the Emperor wrote back to King Oscar, noting the King's statement that he had no plans for conquest and that he intended to follow strictly and impartially his proclaimed neutrality, and taking this as at least partly the assurance he had asked for.[cxlix] On 15th March, the Swedish cabinet was informed that all powers (with the exception of Brazil, whose reply was still lagging) had accepted the Swedish neutrality.[cl]

Two further points need to be made in this chapter. First, the Swedish negotiations, both with Denmark and later with the other foreign powers, clearly show the dominant role of the King in setting foreign policy. It is true that Swedish diplomats were involved in the negotiations the whole time. But all Swedish sources make it clear that the diplomatic establishment was generally pro-Russian or at least favoured sticking to the policy of 1812.[cli] Nevertheless, the Swedish neutrality and the form it took marked a clear break with this policy. That was clearly the aim and doing of the King. In fact, it is clear that the King aimed to make decisions alone and was careful not to let his ministers know too much of what he planned to do.[clii] Perhaps the best illustration is a note from the King to Baron Manderström, the State Secretary for Foreign Affairs and hence the second-ranking member of the Foreign Office. The note is dated 24th October 1853, ie when negotiations with Denmark were well under way:

"His Ex. Sparre [Prime Minister for Justice and temporarily in charge of foreign affairs] asked me last week whether I would not announce in the Cabinet that I, in conjunction with the King of Denmark, have resolved in the case of an outbreak of fighting, to observe a strict neutrality. To this I replied that I had nothing against informing the ministers of the decision I had taken; this could conceivably occur the same day I arrive or at Thursday's cabinet meeting. Please give His Ex. my regards and show him these lines."[cliii]

Second, was Swedish neutrality really so strict and impartial? Already at this stage there were signs that Swedish policy was tilting in a pro-Allied direction. To give but a few examples: Notwithstanding Swedish surprise and dismay that their Declaration of Neutrality was treated differently from the Danish one, there were, in fact, differences between them. A crucial one and certainly of importance to the Allies, was that while Danish ports were closed to *all* ships from the warring powers, the Swedish closure only referred to *warships* – transports could enter any Swedish port. Already in March 1853, the Swedish Prime Minister for Foreign Affairs, Baron Stierneld, had told the Danish Minister to Stockholm, Count Scheel-Plessen, that King Oscar would maintain a strict neutrality as long as possible, but that if he had to deviate from this policy, he would turn his arms against Russia ("guerre avec la Russie le plus tard possible, avec l'Angleterre jamais" – "war with Russia as late as possible, with England never").[cliv] Already in January 1854, Sir William Grey, the British Chargé d'Affaires in Stockholm, could report that Crown Prince Karl kept supplying him with information about the situation in Sweden and in Finland, with maps over fortified positions and naval charts, all of which found their way to the British Admiralty.[clv] Moreover, even as the Swedish government was telling its Russian counterparts that – following the closure of the inner harbours in Slite and Karlsten to foreign warships – there were no Swedish ports suitable for deep-drafted warships, Stierneld had instructed Rehausen to inform the British cabinet that there were a number of suitable ports available and that even in the closed ports, the outer harbour would remain open.[clvi]

Nor were the Allies uninterested. As early as 29thth December 1853, the French Foreign Minister Edouard Droyun de Lhuys had suggested to the Count Moltke, Danish Minister in Paris, an offensive/defensive alliance between Denmark, Sweden and the Allies. Moltke's impression, reported to his government, was that Droyun de Lhuys had greater hopes of an alliance with Sweden than with Denmark.[clvii] This seems to have been the first indication of an Allied interest in a Nordic alliance. It would not be the last.

As the year 1854 dawned and war approached, the stage in the Baltic region thus included two neutrals, one of which was already tilting towards the Allies. On the Allied side, their war-plans included operations in the Baltic. But Britain lacked the resources to fight a two-front war on land and sea, and France was barely able to do so.[clviii] An alliance with Sweden – on the right terms – therefore held a clear attraction.

Chapter 3: 1854: 1st Baltic Expedition and failed negotiations

In early 1854, before war was declared, Britain sent a naval squadron to the Baltic, with the aim of bottling up or – ideally – destroying the Russian Baltic fleet and blockading the Russian coast. Part of the commander's instructions were to, if necessary, protect, and ideally also cooperate with, Sweden. During the year, both France and Great Britain approached the King of Sweden with a view to concluding an offensive alliance. The Baltic campaign was at best a qualified success. The alliance negotiations foundered, but a foundation had been laid for renewed attempts in 1855. This chapter looks at the background to the Baltic Expedition, with special attention given to the role potentially played by Sweden in Allied plans and discussions. It then briefly covers the operations in the Baltic and finally looks in depth at the negotiations and argues that they failed, partly because of the weak Allied showing in the Baltic, but mainly because the Allies were not prepared to pay Sweden's price for an alliance; and Sweden was not prepared to change its terms.

The idea of attacking Russia in the Baltic did not suddenly appear in 1854. On the contrary, there is considerable evidence that at least the British Admiralty had for some time realised that a war with Russia mainly would have to take place at sea; and that, if so, the Baltic Sea would by necessity become a theatre of war. Moreover, since the 1840s the Royal Navy was wedded to a 'Cherbourg Strategy', ie a strategy based on forestalling a (French) invasion by destroying the main French naval base.[clix] Applying this to Russia meant attacking the Russian Black Seas Fleet in Sevastopol and the Baltic Fleet in Sveaborg and Kronstadt. In August and September 1853, Sir James Graham, First Lord of the Admiralty, sent Captain John Washington, an officer "of a first-rate ability as a surveyor", to visit both Kronstadt and the Åland Islands.[clx] Royle claims that

Graham was very keen on getting Sweden to join the Allies, referring to 'my darling project of a northern maritime confederacy against Russia'.[clxi] According to Royle, Graham was convinced that a stunning naval victory in the Baltic was the way to achieve this, and wanted reward Sweden for its support with Finland. This would put paid to Russian naval ambitions in the Baltic, which was Britain's main concern. Lambert claims that Graham officially played down the Baltic theatre, but unofficially pushed for a display of British power there and for the Swedish recovery of Finland. In contrast to Royle, Lambert gives a source for Graham's quote (letter to Lord Clarendon dated 28th February 1854).[clxii] But the weight ostensibly given to the Baltic is somewhat undermined by the surprising ignorance shown by Graham and the Admiralty of the Baltic (in spite of Captain Washington's mission) and of Swedish neutrality (eg, expecting the Royal Navy to be able to hire Swedish pilots or even officers).[clxiii] On the other hand, the Admiralty's instructions to Admiral Sir Charles Napier who commanded the British squadron in the 1854 Baltic campaign, did include that he was to protect Swedish and Danish ships and territory from a Russian attack, should the governments of these countries request him to do so.[clxiv] They may have contained more than that in terms of a possible Swedish alliance. Earp states that Napier was supposed to "look to Åland" as bait for Sweden to join the war.[clxv] He also claims that the British Government expected Napier's squadron to be reinforced by France and Sweden, as it would otherwise be difficult to see what could be achieved in the Baltic.[clxvi] However, Earp's book is very much a defence of Napier's behaviour during the 1854 Baltic Expedition in the face of official criticism following the perceived failure of the campaign, and has to be treated with some scepticism.

But there is other evidence that a Swedish alliance early on figured in the minds of British decision-makers. The earliest approach from the Allies to the King of Sweden took place on 15th June 1854, when two French officers met him on Gotland and proposed an alliance, but as early as 20th May, 1854, Lord John Russell, at this stage Leader of the House of Commons, circulated a memorandum to the Cabinet outlining the case for an alliance with Sweden.[clxvii] This (including the Cabinet response) will be addressed further below, in connection with the Allied-Swedish negotiations. First, however, it is necessary to outline the 1854 Baltic campaign. This is important, because the campaign, its successes and failures and its conduct, were all relevant to Sweden's willingness or otherwise to take part in the war.

In early 1854, there were bright hopes for the Baltic Expedition. As noted above (p. 5), the British squadron set sail for the Baltic before the war began, with the British ultimatum to Russia timed to expire as soon as the Royal Navy could reach Reval. Earp claims that "Though few in point of numbers, never, perhaps, had finer ships left our shores; yet never before had a squadron sailed so deplorably manned."[clxviii] But the second part of the sentence perhaps betrays the hyperbole in the first part, particularly given Earp's bias. Moreover, he points out that the crew was badly trained[clxix], that there was a lack of pilots, which Sir Charles Napier was supposed to hire in Denmark and Sweden,[clxx] and that it lacked shallow-draught gunboats, a category of ships crucial for operations in the Baltic.[clxxi] The lack of gunboats is also observed by Cullberg, who assumes that this meant that Napier expected help from Sweden's 200 gunboat navy.[clxxii] Runeberg makes the same point, noting how Napier repeatedly asked the Admiralty for gunboats.[clxxiii]

But the Baltic Squadron did not only suffer from a lack of gunboats or pilots, or even experienced crews (although the latter was a problem; a number of collisions between British ships did not impress Swedish and Danish onlookers). There were other problems as well. One concerned the character of the commanding officer. Sir Charles Napier was a genuine war hero but given to quarrels and insubordination. Unfortunately, he was also – due to the Navy's seniority rules and the lack of major campaigns since the Napoleonic Wars – about the only Admiral of sufficient seniority to command a squadron, yet not so old that his command was out of the question. Sir James Graham, writing to the Queen to outline the case for appointing Napier to the Baltic command, also expressed clear misgivings about him.[clxxiv]

But a more important issue is what the 1854 Baltic campaign actually aimed at. A fundamental problem was that Britain lacked the resources to fight a two-front war (see page 41). If the Crimea became the primary theatre of war, the Baltic by default became secondary. Greenhill and Giffard claim that the British government never intended to achieve more than it did in 1854, that is to say, impose a blockade on Russia and reconnoitre the Baltic.[clxxv] But this may be an *ex post facto* construction. Although Napier's instructions concentrated on blockading the Gulf of Finland, they also included investigating the possibility of an attack on the three major Russian fortifications in the Baltic, Bomarsund on Åland, Sveaborg outside Helsingfors and Kronstadt guarding the entrance to St Petersburg. Destroying the Russian Baltic Fleet would have been ideal, but the Russians, knowing themselves to be outgunned by the more modern British ships, declined to offer battle, preferring to shelter behind the guns of Sveaborg or Kronstadt. While this meant a strategic success, it was also a bloodless success, and one unlikely to appease the British public.[clxxvi] However, as early as 1st May 1854, the First Lord wrote to Napier, noting that "I by no means contemplate an attack on either Sveaborg or on Cronstadt. I believe them to be all but impregnable from the sea, and none but a very large army could co-operate by land efficiently in presence of such a force as Russia could easily concentrate for the defence of the approaches to her capital."[clxxvii] This is a further indication that Graham expected and hoped for Swedish participation, since only Sweden had the armed forces necessary and available to enable Allies to match the Russian forces. This implies that the British were serious in their negotiations with Sweden, thus addressing one of the research questions.

The story of the 1854 Baltic Campaign is soon told. In mid-June, the Royal Navy squadron was joined by a French squadron under Admiral Parseval-Deschênes, which also carried an expeditionary force of 10,000 soldiers. Over the summer, the Allies attacked a number of Finnish ports, capturing ships and burning supplies (frequently belonging to British merchants and in contravention of their orders, which were to restrict their attacks to shipyards and storehouses[clxxviii]) but otherwise achieving little except strengthening Finnish loyalty to the Russian Empire and alienating the Swedes – possibly beginning with the King.[clxxix] Napier's own investigations and reconnaissance convinced him that without the help of Sweden's gunboat flotilla, he would be unable to take either Sveaborg or Kronstadt.[clxxx] This was not a view necessarily shared by all his subordinates: Brigadier-General Jones reconnoitred Sveaborg and proposed a plan to land troops and artillery on one of the outlying islands off that fortress. But this plan was finally dismissed by an Anglo-French Council of War in September.

The campaign did see one major result, which also played a key role in the negotiations with Sweden. This was the destruction of Bomarsund, a recently built fortress on the Åland Islands. These islands were originally part of Sweden and were conquered by Russia in 1809. Their situation in the middle of the Baltic between Finland and Sweden (see map, p. 112) gives them great strategic value, offensive to Russia, defensive to Sweden. As noted above (p. 5), Lambert claims that the Treaty of Fredrikshamn in 1809 contained a clause demilitarising the islands – a point easily refuted by reading the original text of the Treaty.[clxxxi] In 1832, Russia began to build a large fortress at Bomarsund. Palmstierna claims that, given that Finland is protected by Sveaborg; and that an attack on Sweden just as easily can be done from Åbo – in fact, had to come from there, since it needed steamships for transports and Åland lacks a port – Bomarsund clearly had an offensive purpose.[clxxxii]

Once the Allies had decided that Sveaborg and Kronstadt were impossible to attack, Bomarsund became a logical target. But here, too, the confusion that seems to dog Allied intentions towards the Baltic, comes to the fore. On the one hand, initial allied planning seems to have assumed that Bomarsund could only be taken with Swedish assistance. This is confirmed by a letter from Sir James Graham to Admiral

Napier on 9th May 1854, where he writes "Much depends on the final decision of Sweden. If she will join you with her gunboats and her army, not only Bomarsund, but Sveaborg will be within your power of attack."[clxxxiii] Hamilton also feels that the Allies assumed that Sweden would join the war and help take Bomarsund.[clxxxiv] But others, eg, Jonasson, feel that destroying Bomarsund and taking Åland was intended as bait to Sweden to join the war.[clxxxv] Here too, a letter from Sir James Graham to Sir Charles Napier can be quoted for support. The First Lord writes that that Sweden is well disposed "but wants subsidies and guarantees that we cannot give her." However, he expresses the view that her own interests will eventually compel her to join Great Britain on easier terms, possibly by offering her Åland.[clxxxvi]. Finally, there is French correspondence (see below) that implies that Åland was only to be used to lure Sweden into the war, but this too could be an *ex post facto* reconstruction.

The Allies began to bombard Bomarsund on 8th August. On 16th August, the fortress surrendered. Over the next two weeks, the Allies attempted to induce Sweden to occupy the islands over the winter, but, failing to get a positive response, they destroyed the fortress on 2nd September. The taking of Bomarsund was the main military effect of the 1854 Baltic Campaign. Although the British public hungered for more northern glory and Admiral Napier at one stage contemplated an assault on either Sveaborg or Åbo, the fall of Bomarsund brought the campaign to an end.[clxxxvii] The French and British commanders held a council of war in September, agreeing that there was little more that could be achieved in the Baltic, after which the French squadron sailed home. On 10th October, Admiral Napier admitted that the campaign was over, and the British squadron also left.

Militarily, the 1854 Baltic Campaign achieved little. It did little actual harm to Russia and strengthened the loyalty of its Finnish subjects. But it tied up large numbers of Russian troops (up to 300,000 men) in the area, which otherwise could have been sent to the Crimea and potentially changed the course of the war there.[clxxxviii] It also formed the background against which the negotiations between the Allies and Sweden took place.

It has already been made clear that some British politicians had entertained thoughts of somehow bringing Sweden into the war against Russia. Similar ideas had clearly been current in France had. As it happened, the first *formal* approach to the King of Sweden and Norway was French. But there were previous *informal* approaches as well as internal discussions, at least within the British government.

The first direct approach to Sweden came from France. On 5th April, 1854, Victor Lobstein, the French Minister to Stockholm, was received by the King and presented a despatch from Foreign Minister Droyun de Lhuys where the French government expressed the hope that Sweden would take an active part in the conflict and seize the opportunity to recover Finland.[clxxxix] J B Conacher, in *Britain and the Crimea: Problems of War and Peace*, claims that this irritated the British government, which felt it should have been consulted.[cxc] Baumgart feels that one reason the British government initially was less keen on a Swedish alliance is that, as the junior partner in the alliance with France, it feared that its role and influence would be diluted if the alliance were expanded.[cxci] At this stage, the King referred to his recently issued Declaration of Neutrality which he felt honour-bound to maintain. Moreover, since both Britain and France had proclaimed that they had no desire for territorial aggrandisement, he did not feel that Sweden could go to war with the express aim of enlarging its territory. This being said, he stressed that he was only referring to the current situation and that nobody could know what the future held. Should Sweden be obliged to take part in the war, it could raise some 120,000 troops, of which 60-70,000 would be available for foreign service. Finally, the King made it clear that he was not prepared to act without Austria.[cxcii] This opening episode is interesting, partly because of a subsequent event. In the spring of 1854, Admiral Virgin, Sweden's Minister to the Court of St James, had asked for a meeting with Lord Clarendon to notify him that the Swedish Neutrality Declaration had come into force. The Foreign Secretary brought up the issue of Finland and asked if a return of Swedish rule would be welcomed. Virgin disclaimed any first-hand knowledge, but said that in his view, recovering Finland back would be "peu désirable pour ma patrie" ("little to wish for my country"), to which Lord Clarendon replied "You are absolutely right, Monsieur; you would thus be too close to Russia and would always have to be vigilant."[cxciii] This was a striking example of how the Swedish foreign policy establishment was not in the King's confidence and worked at cross-purposes with him; and Runeberg notes that Virgin was subsequently reprimanded by King Oscar.[cxciv]

The next approach seems to have been Admiral Napier's audience with King Oscar on 25th April 1854. Napier's squadron had reached Älvsnabben outside Stockholm and the Admiral visited the Swedish capital, where he was received by the King. The King's personal notes from this audience state that Napier noted that Britain would not be content with Russia evacuating the Danube Principalities, but must secure a safer future. He went on to say that the struggle must primarily be fought in the North, where this goal could be achieved. But for this, a land army was needed, namely the Swedish one. The King agreed and replied that, at the right time, he would throw 60,000 men into the balance. But there were dangers to this course and he feared for the inheritance that it would leave his descendants. (Here, the King referred to the likelihood that a vengeful Russia would be more than likely to try to retake Finland once Britain and France had made peace and left Sweden to its own devices. This was to be a recurring Swedish concern, although one never addressed in terms of trying to receive guarantees for the future.) In addition, Sweden would need subsidies to go to war. Napier responded that he was not empowered to propose a treaty. In spite of Napier's opening comments, the King pointed out that the question was not yet what he would call a European one, which would justify him to deviate from his neutral position. He also raised the question of Austria's position.[cxcv]

The King's reply to Napier is important for a number of reasons. First, it establishes that the King was willing to join the war *under the right conditions*. This already goes beyond his reply to Lobstein. Had he been opposed to joining under any circumstances, he could just as easily again have referred to his neutral status, the recently issued Neutrality Declaration and left the topic at that. Second, we find early expression of two of the conditions for joining that King Oscar repeatedly will return to over the coming 18 months: The war must be a European war rather than a Near Eastern one (in other words, its aim must be to stop Russia's advancing power, rather than solely defending Turkey against Russia); and Austria must join the war. Judging by the King's notes, Sweden was serious about joining the Crimean War, albeit on its own terms – going a long way to answering one of the research questions.

However, this begs the question as to how much we can trust King Oscar's notes. It can probably be assumed that the King wrote his notes for a number of reasons – as an *aide memoire* for himself; in order to help his successors on the Swedish throne in future situations where this knowledge might be useful; and, at least likely, with a view to posterity. But these are his private notes. He is unlikely to have assumed that they would be scrutinised by future researchers. In the absence of indications to the contrary, it therefore should be assumed that the King faithfully recorded the truth – as he saw and remembered it.

Some of the other sources elaborate on Napier's audience with the King. Greenhill & Giffard claim that Napier asked the King for the use of Sweden's archipelagic fleet, a request that was denied.[cxcvi] This addresses another of the research questions, namely, why the Allies would want Sweden to join the war. Apart from the obvious attraction of another ally, the request – if made – highlights one of Sweden's key assets, its 200 gunboats. Although the alleged request is not repeated in any other source, it would fit in with the fact that Napier had repeatedly urged the Admiralty to build small gunboats and steamers for use in the Baltic[cxcvii] Earp claims that Napier offered the King the use of his (ie, Napier's) services, should the King wish to avail himself of them, but that the King changed the subject and stressed his desire for neutrality.[cxcviii] But Earp also mentions the King's condition that the war should become European, not just Turkish, which somewhat argues against the view that the King dismissed Swedish participation.[cxcix] Hallendorff seems to support Greenhill & Giffard by noting that these efforts to entice the King to join the Allies were damaged by Napier's admission that, in fact, he was the one who needed assistance.[cc] Eriksson claims that the King informed both Napier and the French Minister Lobstein that he knew that the Allies wanted Swedish assistance – but he did not know how far they were prepared to go and what to pay for it. However, the King stressed that a decisive blow could only be directed against Russia's Baltic provinces and with the assistance of Sweden's army and its brown-water navy.[cci]

A further argument in favour of the view that the King was seriously considering participation in the war is that soon after Napier's audience, the Swedish government asked the Austrian government about its intentions. The British Minister, Sir William Grey reported to Lord Clarendon that someone (not named in the dispatch, but, judging by the description, clearly Crown Prince Karl) had told him that the King expected the reply to be one favouring joint Swedish-Austrian action against Russia, one in the north and one in the south.[ccii]

Following Napier's audience with King Oscar, Sir William Grey had an audience with King Oscar on 16th May. Grey put forward the argument that Swedish war participation would have a positive effect on Germany, notably on the King of Prussia, who was vacillating, as well as ensure that Austria became a belligerent. The King, presumably concerned at what he perceived to be a lack of British interest in his terms for an alliance, tried to frighten Grey by explaining how Russia, by occupying the Scandinavian peninsula would gain another 50-60,000 excellent sailors and good ports within 1,000 kilometres from the English Channel. In his report to Lord Clarendon, Grey noted that he felt there was a danger of letting a splendid opportunity to block Russia's ambitions slip by.[cciii] But the Cabinet was less enthusiastic. On 20th May 1854, Lord John Russell, at this stage Leader of the House of Commons, sent a memorandum to his colleagues in the Cabinet, writing:

There are two subjects connected with the conduct of the war which it is very desirable that the Cabinet should consider without loss of time. The first is the separation of the office of Secretary of State for the Colonies from that of Secretary of State for the War Department. ... The next subject still more urgent is that of a subsidy & treaty of alliance with Sweden. The King of Sweden, it appears by the last accounts is more anxious on this question than ever, & is confident of the support of his government [illegible] if rest of the present ministers ...... It will require six weeks after the signature of a treaty before the Swedish army can be ready for action. Supposing the treaty can be signed by the 19th of June the Swedish army would not [be ready?] before the 1st of August. Hardly sufficient time for operations will be left and unless instructions are sent in a week the season will be lost. ... A land force is essential in the Baltic. ... I therefore propose that official instructions be sent at once to Mr Grey empowering him to sign I A treaty of alliance without guarantee of conquests II A treaty of subsidy, half the subsidy to be paid by England and half by France.[cciv]

However, the Cabinet was divided. Lord Clarendon (the Foreign Secretary) was positive, stressing the usefulness and low cost of Sweden's army, but was not prepared to give any guarantees for the future – adding that he did not feel the French government would be prepared to do so either.[ccv] Sir William Molesworth (First Commissioner of Works) preferred to concentrate on the Black Sea. If Sweden were prepared to join of her own bat, Britain could guarantee that she would not lose any territory, and if she could conquer anything it would be up to her to keep it.[ccvi] William Gladstone (Chancellor of the Exchequer) did not like the idea of paying subsidies and preferred to bring Austria into the war.[ccvii] Sir Charles Wood (later 1st Viscount Halifax, President of the Board of Control) queried the objectives of the war and noted that Sweden's objective was to recover Finland.[ccviii] Sidney Herbert (Secretary at War) was more positive and referred to the importance of destroying Sveaborg and Kronstadt as being on par with the destruction of Sevastopol. He hoped Sweden would be prepared to accept Britain's terms for an alliance.[ccix] Finally, Lord Palmerston (Home Secretary) was keener, stressing the importance of destroying Sveaborg and Kronstadt.[ccx] However, with only Russell and Palmerston feeling sufficiently strongly about the move and Clarendon half-hearted, the idea was dropped. Britain now took a back seat in the negotiations with Sweden.

Instead, the French government came to the fore. On 29th May, the King received Lobstein, who reported that his government had every reason to believe that Austria was imminently going to declare for the western powers; and that the French Emperor still hoped that Sweden would join the war once Austria openly has declared itself. In his reply, the King pointed out that the conclusion of a treaty between Austria and Prussia on 20th April, did not give the reason to believe that Austria would join the Allies to limit Russia's power. Under these circumstances, he saw no reason to abandon his neutrality. However, if he were to do so, his conditions would be the following: The war would have to be declared to be a war for the balance of power in Europe; Austria had to join the war; no country would make a separate peace until the guarantees necessary to safeguard the future of Europe had been reached, and these were to include Austrian possession of the Danubian Principalities and Swedish recovery of Finland. However, if these conditions were accepted, he would consider the Allied offer and – if he decided to act – act with all power and without hesitation. However, time was of the essence.[ccxi] The King also made a point of stating that he felt he could set out conditions; after all he had not approached the Allies with dreams of expansion, they had approached him.[ccxii]

On 15th June 1854, whilst inspecting the reinforcements and fortifications on the island of Gotland in the Baltic, the King was approached by two French emissaries, Major Blanchard and Captain Karth. The two French officers conveyed the Emperor Napoleon's interest in proper guarantees for European future; and mentioned a French army of 100,000 men that was being gathered in St Omer, ready for use in the Baltic. They implied that France would welcome the opportunity of staging the army in a friendly country not too far from the theatre of war, and Major Blanchard specifically asked if the French troops could winter in Sweden, so as not to have to return the long way home. He also asked for the right to purchase horses and supplies in Sweden. The King countered the request for winter quarters by suggesting the conquest of a *pied à terre* in enemy territory, eg, Åland, Sveaborg or the island of Ösel off the coast of Estonia, noting that there would be little point in making a conquest that would have to be abandoned in the winter. As for horses, the Allies were welcome to approach Swedish tradesmen, but they were more likely to find good mounts in Denmark.[ccxiii] Ostensibly, Blanchard and Karth had a limited mission. However, Hallendorff surmises that their real aim was to ascertain what Sweden's price for joining the Allies would be.[ccxiv]

Following the King's visit to Gotland, Sir William Grey reported that the King seemed more 'anglomane' than ever and more ill-disposed towards Russia than usual.[ccxv] This is ostensibly contradicted by a letter from Albert Ehrensvärd, First Secretary of the Swedish Foreign Office to Baron Manderström, where he wrote that "The King seems to me to be fairly peacefully inclined and not intending on abandoning the neutrality. Prince Oscar speaks broadly in the same manner so that the war policy is only championed by the Crown Prince."[ccxvi] However, Grey's reading of the King is supported by the fact that he and other diplomats were invited to observe a manoeuvre of the Swedish gun-boat flotilla on board the King's steamer *Valkyrian*. Grey reports that both the King and the Crown Prince gave the impression that they intended to join the Western Powers as soon as time was ripe. The King is quoted as saying: "If a combined English, French and Swedish army can begin a campaign in Finland before 1st September, the war will be over before Christmas." Crown Prince Karl asked the British envoy (referring to the gunboats): "Do you not think these would be of some service to you?" Grey replied: "that I hoped it would not be long before they were put to the test." Meanwhile, the King's second son Prince Oscar, Duke of Östergötland (the future King Oscar II) asked him: "What do you think of our forces? We are only recruits, but this is very good exercise for what I hope will soon be a reality. But do not let us lose time - the summer is very short."[ccxvii]

Meanwhile, there are further indications that the British government was getting less keen on a Swedish alliance. In late June Lord Cowley, the British Ambassador to France, met Foreign Minister Droyun de Lhuys and suggested that it was no longer suitable to pressure King Oscar, as the King would not listen to anything until the position of Austria had become clear. Droyun de Lhuys replied that the Allied governments could still work on a treaty proposal, including a monthly subsidy of 5 million francs, 50,000 Anglo-French troops and a guarantee that Swedish interests would be safeguarded in peace. In exchange for this, Sweden should contribute 60,000 troops and 200 gunboats. All this was somewhat less than King asked but the difference was very small. However, the promise of a recovery of Finland was replaced by vague guarantee which Runeberg feels that King Oscar would not have accepted – but he also believes that Britain would not in any case have guaranteed a recovery of Finland.[ccxviii]

The French persevered, however. On 23 July Blanchard and Lobstein again met the King. Blanchard had in the meantime been to Vienna and been received by the Austrian Emperor Franz Josef. Blanchard claimed that the latter had nothing to object to about Sweden's desired guarantees and promised to accept whatever Napoleon III did to achieve this goal. According to King Oscar's diary notes, the King replied that all he got was an indication that Austria would join the Allies, not a guarantee, whereas Lobstein and Blanchard claim the King said he was convinced and assured by Franz Josef's reported words.[ccxix] Whether or not the King was convinced, he did – through Manderström – propose a treaty text, namely: First, France and England declare in a treaty that the object of the started war is to make Russia less dangerous for the future of Europe; second, that they see a necessary guarantee for this to be Finland's detachment from Russia and union with Sweden; third, that they undertake to pursue this goal with the necessary forces by land and by sea; fourth, that peace with Russia only be concluded after internal agreement by all powers signatory to the treaty; fifth, that Austria formally subscribe to the basic principles in this treaty; sixth, that the King of Sweden & Norway immediately be invited by the three powers to accede to the treaty as an equal; and seventh, that other issues, eg, subsidies be treated in separate articles. In addition, the King orally noted that he would need subsidies of 3.3 million Riksdaler banco (£275,000) per month in order to maintain 70,000 troops by land or sea, 200 brown-water ships, four ships of the line and two gun frigates, in addition, to another 3-4 million (£250,000 - £335,000) for preparatory armaments. Overall, the King's attitude was very much that he wanted to make absolutely clear what he demanded for Swedish participation in order to avoid attempts to drag Sweden into war before safe guarantees were received.[ccxx]

Notwithstanding the King's insistence on Austrian participation in the war as pre-condition for Swedish belligerency, the French continued their efforts. On 26th July, Lobstein had a new audience with the King, where he proposed signing an immediate treaty on the basis outlined by the King, but excluding the point about Austrian participation, replacing it with a clause saying that the treaty would only enter into force once Austria had acceded to it. The King rejected this and in fact raised his demands, insisting on supreme command in the northern theatre, unless the Emperor Napoleon were present, in which case command should be joint between them.[ccxxi] But he continued to give the impression of being willing to go to war. On 29th July, he gave an audience at the Haga Palace to the commanders of the French expeditionary force, Generals Baraguey d'Hilliers and Niel. The King told them that he would need two months to assemble 60,000 men and transport them on Allied ships to Finland; and that he would need substantial subsidies to join the war. However, he also noted that as long as Russia kept St Petersburg, it could easily attack Finland once the Allies were gone. The allied troops were needed, since Russia could raise 150,000 troops in the north. Finally, the King made it clear that he understood a campaign in the north to be conditional on the campaign in the south being victorious.[ccxxii]

As has been shown, King Oscar tied Sweden's position to that of Austria. This was partly in order to ensure that the war against Russia would achieve the broadest possible basis, geographically as well as nationally. It would not only mean that Russia could not concentrate all its resources on one front, but also that reversing a peace settlement would become more difficult the more powers were involved. But, as has been briefly covered in Chapter 1 (p. 21f), Austria was the least likely power to go to war. Could it therefore be that tying Sweden's policy to Austria's was a way for the King of hiding his true intentions and that he intended never to go to war? Alternatively, was the King – like the French and the British – misled by a skilful Austrian policy of always promising but never fulfilling?

In early May 1854 King Oscar asked the Swedish Minister to Austria, General Carl von und zu Mansbach[ccxxiii] to inform the Austria government of Sweden's wish to confidentially coordinate its policy with Austria. Mansbach was to inform the Austrians that as long as the war was about the Eastern Question, Sweden would remain neutral. But if Austrian interests demanded an extension of the conflict, King Oscar was prepared to reconsider this stance. The Austrian Foreign Minister Buol replied that it would be difficult for Sweden to keep neutrality if conflict expanded, but advised it to stick to neutrality as long as it could, adding "If, however, this attitude were to prove impossible to maintain, the King's government could have full confidence in Austria's eagerness to use its entire influence in support of the demands that the Swedish government were to set out for such a sacrifice."[ccxxiv] The King clearly saw this as Austrian support for a Swedish recovery of Finland. But this may be because he was eager to read it this way. General Mansbach also met Prince Metternich, the retired but still hugely influential former Foreign Minister, who advised him that Sweden should stick to its neutrality. It might recover Finland but would then have to garrison a long border with Russia, without having acquired the increased revenues to do so.[ccxxv]

Runeberg feels that King Oscar was given clear signals that Austria wished to dampen Sweden's war fever.[ccxxvi] Whether or not the King understood this is not clear; but his diplomats certainly did, with Manderström expressing the hope that Austrian tardiness would postpone any Swedish decision over the winter.[ccxxvii]

At the same time, there were more signals that the British government was retreating further from its interest in a Swedish alliance. Lord Clarendon told the Swedish Minister to the Court of St James, Admiral Virgin, that he had full sympathy with Sweden's fragile position and never understood what use Swedish participation in the war could be to the Allies unless Austria joined as well (causing Virgin to write to Manderström that Britain wished to leave Sweden alone).[ccxxviii] In early August 1854, Clarendon repeated his views to M. Baudin, the French Chargé d'Affaires in London, expressing doubts about the wisdom of taking Finland from Russia. This would leave Russia humiliated and also force Sweden to constantly guard a long border difficult to defend.[ccxxix] The British government also repeatedly made it clear that it was not going to guarantee a Swedish recovery of Finland, which might prolong a war that had reached a satisfactory conclusion elsewhere.[ccxxx] However, Baudin – who was under instructions to urge the Lord Clarendon to press Austria precisely in order to enable a Swedish alliance – also claimed on 12th August that the British Foreign Secretary had agreed to the following: A treaty to be concluded with Austria which would not mention Finland. The Swedish government would be offered to accede to this treaty, following which the Swedish contingent for the campaign in Finland would be specified in a later military convention. The Allies would then offer non-binding guarantees regarding Sweden's expansion in Finland – possibly saving this for an official Note. The question of the exact nature of Sweden's relationship to its regained province (personal union, as between Sweden and Norway, or a return to the pre-1809 situation with Finland as an integral part of Sweden) would be tabled for later resolution.[ccxxxi] However, judging by King Oscar's attitude during this period, it is unlikely that these vague assurances would have been enough to satisfy him.

The negotiations between the Allies and Sweden seemed to have reached an impasse, when a new factor suddenly revived them. This was the fall of Bomarsund. Whereas previously there had been some thought in the Allied camp that Bomarsund could only be taken with Swedish assistance, the thought now arose that the Åland Islands could be used to inveigle Sweden into joining the war. Immediately following the Russian surrender of the fortress, a French officer (Captain Melin, ADC to General Baraguey d'Hilliers) was sent to Stockholm to offer the King possession of the islands. The French army, still traumatised by its experience in Russia in 1812/1813, was not keen to winter in the Baltic.[ccxxxii] However, if Sweden was prepared to garrison Bomarsund, the French expeditionary force was prepared to winter in Sweden. Foreign Minister Droyun de Lhuys telegraphed Lobstein, "Tell the King of Sweden: If you wish to occupy the Åland Islands, we hand them over to you and leave our ten thousand men in Stockholm over the winter. If you do not wish this, we will immediately evacuate the islands after having destroyed the defence works. Send the King's reply directly to General Baraguey d'Hilliers."[ccxxxiii]

The offer of the Åland Islands put the King in a quandary. Occupying the islands would breach Sweden's neutrality and almost certainly bring about war with Russia. This was also very clearly the French intention. When asked what to with Bomarsund, Napoleon III telegraphed to his Minister of War

Jean Baptiste Vaillant "Il faut compromettre la Suede; tachez que ma commande de pelisses ne soit pas inutile." ("Sweden must be compromised; Ensure that my army is not meaningless.") Droyun de Lhuys slightly altered the Imperial command but instructed Lobstein "Il faut mettre le roi Oscar en demeure de garder notre prise. Compromettre la Suede est le seul but de l'expedition." ("King Oscar must be pushed into [actually, dunned into] guarding our prize. Compromising Sweden is the sole object of this expedition.")[ccxxxiv] Claiming that the sole object of the Baltic Campaign was to lure Sweden into the Allied camp (or perhaps rather, force it to break with Russia) is most likely disingenuous and a consequence of the campaign's lack of success.

Unsurprisingly, the King saw through the French attempts. Moreover, his attitude is unlikely to have been improved by Baraguey d'Hilliers' acknowledgement that the camp at St Omer only had 10,000 soldiers, not the 50,000 or 100,000 previously claimed. Eriksson quotes an article in *Indepéndence Belge*, whose Hamburg correspondent has the King burst out "Should therefore, after having waited for five months for your troops, my solders *alone* make up the army against Russia and in case of defeat *alone* experience the sufferings that afflict an army retreating through hostile territory?"[ccxxxv] However, his dilemma remained. Instead, he attempted to persuade the Allies to winter in Finland. At a lunch at the Haga Palace on 19th August, he put it to Lobstein and Captain Melin that leaving Åland would demonstrate the Allies' weakness to all Europe. They would be seen as "oiseaux de passage", migrating birds that flee as soon as there is the slightest cold, something that clearly would diminish the value of their alliance.[ccxxxvi] But if the Allies could not make the King change his mind, neither could he make them change theirs. Accordingly, on 2nd September, the Allies destroyed Bomarsund and evacuated the site. Significantly, all this occurred *before* the Allies had even landed in the Crimea.

From a Swedish perspective, the Allied efforts had not been particularly impressive, with the exception of the fall of Bomarsund. Nor did the fighting in the Crimea in the second half of 1854 inspire much confidence.[ccxxxvii] Cullberg claims that after the fall of Bomarsund, the King was torn between occidentalists and Scandinavists on the one hand, and his sense of duty and fear of Russia on the other.[ccxxxviii] But there was also a feeling of opportunity lost. Once the Allied armies were sent to the Crimea, the King realised that the main effort would be made assaulting, as he put it, the giant's little toe, rather than his jugular.[ccxxxix] If he wished to share the booty, he would now have to modify his demands. Hence, he told Sir William Grey's successor as British Minister in Stockholm, Charles Arthur Magenis, that he had never really asked for a guarantee of the recovery of Finland, nor a promise that the Allies would continue the war until Finland had been reconquered. All he had meant – he claimed – was to point out that it was a European interest to diminish Russia's power; and that only by increasing and strengthening Sweden could a counterpoise to Russia be created in the Baltic. Meanwhile, Admiral Virgin told Magenis that the request for the guarantee had been invented by Foreign Minister Stierneld, who was sure that it would be unacceptable to the Allies.[ccxl] While the latter is unlikely to be true, it is another striking illustration of how the King of Sweden and Norway worked at cross-purposes with his government.

As for the Allies, it was precisely the relative failure of the campaign that made them more eager to achieve Swedish belligerency.[ccxli] The British government was perhaps somewhat less keen than the French, although if Sweden was prepared to accept the Allies' conditions or at least substantially moderate her demands, her contribution would be welcome. Lord Clarendon expressed this view at least twice, once in a private letter, where he wrote "The King should be content to abide by the fortunes of war, to come to an agreement with England and France that the object is to limit the power of Russia, and that in furtherance of it, we should desire to see Finland restored to Sweden, and would use our best efforts for it, but that we could make no pledge nor undertake to prolong the war on account of Finland, though we would undertake not to make peace without the interests of

Sweden being consulted and secured." The letter also noted that if Sweden did nothing to assist Britain and France, she must not expect any consideration from them when final arrangements were made.[ccxlii] On 28th October, Clarendon wrote to Magenis, saying that Admiral Virgin, before leaving London, asked him what HMG views were on the co-operation of Sweden with England in the war against Russia. Clarendon replied that the question was easier answered if he could know what the Swedish government thought, as HMG was not going to urge them to do anything contrary to their interests and likely to endanger their safety. "A desire, however, had been manifested at Stockholm to abandon that position, and negotiations with that object, as Admiral Virgin must be well aware, had been commenced, and had been carried to some length, but they had been put a stop to by the King requiring the restoration of Finland should be guaranteed to Sweden and that the Policy of Austria should guide that of Sweden. The first of these conditions was, I said, out of the question for Her Majesty's Government would never give a guarantee without a reasonable expectation of being able to fulfil it, and it was impossible to foresee the events of war, or whether it would be practicable to wrest Finland from Russia and restore it permanently to Sweden..."[ccxliii] Hallendorff claims that Clarendon also told Virgin that the British government was keen to see Sweden join the Allies; that subsidies of £100,000 or 2.5 million francs per month, as much again from the French government could be arranged; and that Sweden would not be left to face Russia alone.[ccxliv]

There is some ambiguity regarding the French attitude. Runeberg writes that the French were less inclined to press the issue of a Swedish occupation of Bomarsund, because they were convinced of King Oscar's negative attitude to this idea.[ccxlv] But he also notes that in the second half of 1854, Droyun de Lhuys still hoped for Swedish participation in the war. However – and crucially – Sweden's policy was tied to Austria's; and the Austrian Foreign Minister Buol pursued a duplicitous policy, aimed solely at allowing Austria to do nothing and reap maximum rewards, all the while making everyone feel that Austria was on their side. Runeberg quotes Metternich as saying that Austria's aim during the Oriental conflict should be to stick spokes in everyone's wheels to ensure no power gains any advantage.[ccxlvi] Hallendorff claims that from the autumn of 1854, the French government stopped showing an active interest in a Swedish alliance, reverting to hints and discrete nudges, mainly because they believed it was bound to happen anyway.[ccxlvii]

However, there are signs that the French were still eager. In a dispatch dated 27th December 1854, the new Swedish Minister to the Court of St James, Baron Carl Hochschild, reported to Foreign Minister Stierneld that the French Ambassador Walewski[ccxlviii] had repeated to him that "we cannot promise anything with regards to Finland but we will do what we can to return her to you. As for subsidies, there isn't the slightest difficulty and you can count on 5 million francs each month."[ccxlix]

As 1854 drew to a close, therefore, the Allies were still at least somewhat interested in a Swedish alliance, but not on Sweden's terms. By contrast, in Sweden, King Oscar began to realise that if he wanted to join the Allies and take part in the war, he would have to change his tactics. In 1854, he had been the one approached by the Allies and able to set his terms. In 1855, he would have to be more active and to at least some extent play the role of suitor himself. In 1855, these attitudes would pave the way for the November Treaty.

Chapter 4: 1855: 2nd Baltic Expedition and the November Treaty

As the year 1855 began, the Allied armies were bogged down in a Crimean stalemate. In January Lord Aberdeen was replaced as British Prime Minister by Lord Palmerston, who seemed likely to intensify the war effort. A new expedition was sent to the Baltic, but – in spite of inflated claims – it achieved even less than its predecessor. In the autumn, Sevastopol fell, leaving the Allies with the question of how to proceed with the war. Paradoxically, both the stalemate in the Crimea and the eventual success, made the Allies more interested in a Swedish alliance.

In Sweden, meanwhile, the shift of the war to the Crimea and the lesser interest of the Allies in a Swedish alliance in late 1854, led to a change in attitude. Previously, King Oscar had been content to let himself be courted by the British and French governments. Now, he actively started to court them. This chapter will show how this increased interest on both sides for an alliance led to the November Treaty between Great Britain, France and the United Kingdoms of Sweden and Norway. The November Treaty has been widely and correctly perceived to lay the groundwork for Swedish participation in the Crimean War. But where previous authors have surmised secret clauses to the Treaty without having any proof, this chapter will for the first time publish a draft treaty, drawn up in King Oscar's own handwriting, which confirms the King's belligerent intentions, and which contains clauses that could potentially have changed 19th Century European history. Finally, the chapter will argue that the November Treaty played a significant role in bringing Russia to the peace table and the Crimean War to a close.

The 1855 Baltic Campaign was more carefully planned than its predecessor. On behalf of the First Sea Lord, Captain John Sulivan had drawn up a paper outlining what was possible to achieve with a naval force alone; what could be achieved by a combined naval and military force; and what force would be needed if the aim solely was to blockade the Russian coast.[ccl] Sulivan's main conclusions were that in order to take Sveaborg, an army of 40,000 men was needed; and that Kronstadt could be successfully assaulted from the north, using mortar boats and floating batteries.[ccli] The latter point again highlights the potential value to the Allies of Sweden's large gunboat flotilla, and helps address one of the research questions, namely what use Sweden could be in the war. In March 1855, Lord Palmerston outlined a policy for the Baltic, expressing the view that it should be possible to do more than just blockade the Russian ports and fleet. As the Russian fleet was concentrated at Kronstadt, there was no point in attacking Reval or Sveaborg, since success would achieve little and failure would be a disaster. Moreover, the lack of troops to send to the Baltic meant that it would be better to concentrate on the Crimea.[cclii] Palmerston's conclusion meant that the Baltic once again was a secondary theatre. However, the squadron sent was considerably more powerful than its predecessor. The 1854 expedition consisted of 22 vessels with 2,000 guns and 21,800 men.[ccliii] In 1855 the Baltic squadron under Admiral Sir Richard Dundas consisted of 99 warships, all of them steam-driven, with 3,100 guns and 24,000 men, including 3,000 marines.[ccliv] In contrast to 1854, the squadron included gunboats and mortar vessels. In addition, there was yet again a French squadron. After a quiet beginning, mainly restricted to minor landings and raids, activity picked up from July with descents on Finnish towns.[cclv] A reconnaissance of Kronstadt in early June showed that the fortress had been reinforced and convinced Dundas that it could not be successfully assaulted in "the absence of a powerful and numerous [light-draught] flotilla, sufficient to oppose that of the enemy".[cclvi] This again shows the value to the Allies of Sweden's powerful Swedish gunboat flotilla. Left with little to show for their efforts, the Allies decided to bombard Sveaborg to show some initiative.[cclvii]

The bombardment of Sveaborg took place from 9th to 11th August. There is a strange divide in the reporting of the results. Royle and Lambert claim that Sveaborg was destroyed.[cclviii] Bonner-Smith includes documents referring to reports from civilians claiming that the Russian minimising of the effect on Sveaborg was untrue.[cclix] By contrast, Baumgart and Greenhill & Giffard claim that the bombardment achieved little.[cclx] Cullberg goes further and notes that the result – 62 Russian dead and 33 British – not only failed to impress Finns and Swedes but actually produced the opposite effect.[cclxi] Contemporary reports – Finnish newspapers and the memoirs of Posthumus (Johan Carl Hellberg) both agree that the damage was minimal.[cclxii] This is also the impression from a visit to Sveaborg, which shows little, if any reconstruction of buildings that would have been damaged if the allied bombardment really had destroyed the fortress.

Could the Swedish navy have made a difference in the assault on Sveaborg? After all, the Allies had sent gunboats this time and still did not manage to cause significant damage to the fortress. But numbers give a clue. The British squadron had 50 gunboats and mortar boats. The French squadron was smaller.[cclxiii] The attack used 16 gunboats and 16 mortar-boats.[cclxiv] At this stage the Swedish navy had 6 mortar-boats, 122 gunboats and 97 other smaller gun vessels.[cclxv] The Norwegian navy had an additional 129 gunboats of different size.[cclxvi] The waters around Sveaborg are relatively open. Sheer numbers thus imply that the Scandinavian gunboats could have been helpful.

In September and October, the Allied squadrons left the Baltic and the campaign was over. *The Times* was critical of the Baltic efforts, noting that the two campaigns had cost £20 million, with no result except the destruction of Bomarsund and of some stores at Sveaborg.[cclxvii] This is unfair. The Russian merchant fleet had been destroyed and Imperial Navy had been holed up in its bases, unable to threaten either British or French territory. Moreover, Russia had tied up to 300,000 troops and large amounts of material in the Baltic, resources which otherwise could have been sent to the Crimea. But these were passive results. They did not advance the course of the war. Moreover, following the fall of Sevastopol, there was little the Allies could do in the Crimea. If they advanced into Russia, their lines of communication and supply lengthened, while Russia's shortened. If they did nothing, they would eventually have to withdraw, in which case Russia would soon return and rebuild Sevastopol and their Black Sea fleet. If the war were to continue, the Baltic then became the focal point, if only by default.

Nonetheless, in early 1855, the impression from a Swedish horizon was one of concentration on the Crimea. If King Oscar really intended to remain neutral, this was all to the good. However, if he intended to join the war, some way had to be found to refocus attention on the northern theatre. Moreover, this had to be done without appearing too anxious, since that would lower the potential price the King could extract in return for Scandinavian participation in the war. This was even more complicated as the Allies had in the meantime gained a new partner – Sardinia – whose troops were actually helpful in the Crimea.; and who did not require any subsidies. To achieve this aim, the King made extensive use of foreign press and personal intermediaries. This was typical of the King's method of conducting foreign policy. Cullberg notes that throughout 1854 the heads of the Swedish/Norwegian legations in Paris and London were left without instructions regarding the main issues of the day, while the King handled foreign policy personally.[cclxviii] Instead of using the foreign policy establishment, the King relied on personal friends, such as the writer and politician Count David Frölich, Baron Knut Bonde, the Head of the Royal Theatre, and the writer, businessman and politician Gustaf Lallerstedt, as well as on people like the Swedish Count Nils Barck, who was a personal friend of Napoleon III.[cclxix] There were others as well. In Swedish research on this period, they are known as the 'camarilla'. These persons communicated with each other using simple ciphers and code words (King Oscar was Pappa, Napoleon III was Frère, Britain, France and Austria were Anna, Marie and Fanny, Lord Palmerston was called Vega and

Lord Clarendon Daddy; soldiers were *moutons* – sheep.[cclxx]). A typical example of their modus operandi occurred in early 1855. In late February or early March, Baron Bonde informed a Swede living in Paris, Lieutenant Ludvik Lilliehöök, a personal friend of Count Barck, that the Sweden desired closer relations with France. Lilliehöök brought this letter to the attention of Count Charles Tascher de la Pagerie, Chamberlain to the Empress Eugenie and second cousin to the Swedish Queen Josephine, who, in turn, brought it to the eyes of the Emperor.[cclxxi] (One wonders why Bonde needed to use such circuitous routes. His own connections were extremely good; his first wife had been Lady Augusta Fitz-Clarence, a granddaughter of King William IV; his second wife Florence Robinson, was a childhood friend of the Empress Eugenie.[cclxxii]) The signal that there were powerful interests in Sweden that still worked and hoped for a closer relationship with the Allies, was not lost on the French. Through the camarilla, the King worked assiduously to place articles in foreign press, designed to highlight the importance of the Baltic area and the usefulness of a Swedish alliance.

Initially, these approaches seemed successful. On 14th April 1855, Bonde received a telegram from Barck, reporting that the French Emperor had agreed to all the Swedish demands – with the exception of providing troops, since there were none.[cclxxiii] This was repeated by the Emperor to Barck on 30th April. But the provision of 60-70,000 Allied troops was a key condition for Sweden; and since without an Anglo-French expeditionary force there could be no attack on Finland or – more importantly – on St Petersburg, this was tantamount to rejecting the Swedish demands.[cclxxiv] Although Barck made a final appeal to the Emperor for French troops, pointing out that Denmark and the smaller German states were likely to join the war as well, reducing the numbers needed (and holding out the promise of a revolt in Finland – "la levée immediate de 30,000 brave Finlandais" – "the immediate rising of 30,000 brave Finns", a highly unlikely event given Finnish resentment at the Allied depredations), henceforth he began to lose faith in his mission.[cclxxv]

The problem with the Bonde-Barck diplomacy was that the French Emperor lacked the means to fulfil King Oscar's conditions.[cclxxvi] Moreover, where in 1854, the French government had been more interested than the British government in a Swedish alliance, in 1855, the roles were reversed. This was partly due to a change in attitude towards the war. For France, the war was becoming a financial and political burden. Hallendorff shows that the problem was that there could be no acceptable peace unless Sevastopol was taken. But if Sevastopol did not fall (or if it did and Russia did not agree to peace), the Baltic would become the only alternative theatre. Yet, sending a fleet without an army was not going to have an effect. Hence, Sweden again became interesting, at the very least as a staging ground. But this would also involve prolonging the war. For Napoleon, the moment of using Sweden was now past. However, if Sweden could be committed as point of pressure without going to war, that might be a good idea.[cclxxvii]

In addition to the disappointing news from Paris, King Oscar also had to worry about the Vienna Peace Conference, which had opened on 15th March. If the conference were to lead to peace, there would be no war for Sweden to participate in. Had the King but known, he need not have worried; although the reasons for not having to worry were worrisome in themselves. The Peace Conference had been called on the basis of the Four (actually, Five, see p. 18) Points. But the Austrian Emperor Franz Josef had promised the Russian envoy to Vienna, Prince A M Gorchakov, that Austria would not agree to anything that impaired Russia's honour and sovereignty in the Black Sea – in other words, the Third Point (which limited Russia's naval presence in the Black Sea), and the Fifth Point (which allowed for further demands to be raised).[cclxxviii] Baumgart lays the blame for the failure of the conference squarely on this promise.[cclxxix] In other words, the good news that the Peace Conference was coming to nothing, was due to Austria's double game, the same Austria that the King insisted on take part in the war before Sweden would join. This double game was played out for Sweden as well. On

1st May 1855, a dispatch from General Mansbach referred to a conversation with Count Buol, where the Austrian Foreign Minister had clearly made a belligerent impression. Mansbach writes that should the Vienna Conference break down: "…si je n'ai pas interpreté tout a fait en erreur le language de Comte B., l'Autriche doit etre determiné eventuellement a faire la guerre a la Russie." ("if I did not entirely misinterpret the language of Count B. Austria must be determined eventually to make war on Russia").[cclxxx] But this was offset by the news from Barck referred to above, that there were no "*moutons*".

The King's relief at the failure of the Vienna Peace Conference is clear from his diary, where he writes on 12th July, 1855: "As the Four Points failed to lead to a peaceful solution of the war at the Vienna Conference, it seems to be the time to increasingly turn Europe's attention to Nordic issues."[cclxxxi] And further: "On peut envisager comme un grand bonheur pour la cause Européenne et surtout pour l'Empereur Napoléon que la Russia ait par sa resistance empêché les négotations à Vienne d'aboutir." ("One can see it is a great fortune for the European cause and in particular for the Emperor Napoleon, that Russia by its resistance stopped the Vienna negotiations from succeeding.")[cclxxxii] But, at the same time, the King's diary notes begin to become more sceptical of Austria. On 2nd August, 1855, he writes that he finds it difficult to believe that Austria go to war as long as the Allies are stuck outside Sevastopol.[cclxxxiii] Moreover, it was becoming increasingly clear that the French government was only waiting for a decent reason – ideally the fall of Sevastopol – to finish the war. In early September, Baron Bonde wrote in a disillusioned letter to the King from Paris that: "On fera la paix quand on pourra et *comme* on pourra, on stipulera pour *soi*." ("One will make peace when possible and *however* possible and look out for *oneself*.")[cclxxxiv] This is the end of the Bonde-Barck camarilla efforts.

But if France was becoming more inclined to peace, the new British government under Lord Palmerston was becoming more belligerent. Fortunately for the King, he had at his disposal an excellent instrument to attract the attention, not only of the British Government in general, but of the new Prime Minister in particular. This was the issue of the Finnmark and Russia's alleged attempts to secure an ice-free port in northern Norway.

The Finnmark is the north-easternmost part of Norway. In a wider sense, the name applies also to northern Sweden and Finland. The area is sparsely populated, with the inhabitants primarily being the nomadic Sami. Historically, these have tended to ignore the borders drawn up by governments in faraway Stockholm, Copenhagen, Moscow or St Petersburg. In fact, until 1826, a large area – the so-called *Faellesdistrikt* (joint region) was jointly administered by Norway, Russia and Finland. Various treaties, mainly the Treaty of Strömstad of 1751, had over time regulated the traditional use of the land, but, in short, Norwegian Sami would travel south to Finnish pastures in the winter; and Finnish and Russian Sami would travel to the Norwegian coast in the summer to fish, and would leave their boats in Norway over the winter. In 1826, the *Faellesdistrikt* was partitioned between Norway, Finland and Russia. Local Russian protests against this partition later gave rise to British concerns that Russia had tried to seize the entire Finnmark.[cclxxxv] However, there were still outstanding issues left to be regulated, and over the years there were attempts to revise and update the Treaty of 1751. As noted above, in 1836, the British Consul-General in Oslo, John Rice Crowe, wrote a lengthy report to Lord Palmerston on the issue, saying that the Russian government aimed at obtaining an ice-free port in the Varangerfiord in the Finnmark, where they could then build a northern Sevastopol within easy sailing distance of the British Isles. In 1840, there was a proposal to solve the issues by a territorial exchange. King Karl Johan was in favour, but his government opposed the move and managed to stop it. Although the negotiations had been conducted in secret, the Russian Minister leaked the news to his British colleague. The idea that the Russian government had been prepared to give up a strip of land inside Finland in return for a district on the Norwegian coast, seemed to bear out Consul Crowe's concerns.[cclxxxvi] Negotiations continued in a desultory fashion and in 1852, the Finns closed the border for Norwegian Sami.

In spite of this on-going dispute, the Swedish government only briefly touched upon the Finnmark issue over the winter of 1853/54. Instead, it had talked about the Russian threat to the island of Gotland in the Baltic, as well as to the Sound.[cclxxxvii] But in the winter of 1854/55, the Finnmark dispute and Russia's putative plans for a naval base in the North Sea were brought to the fore. This was very much the King's doing. On 12th July, 1855, he wrote in his diary "Already last winter I have third and fourth hand introduced numerous articles aimed at turn the attention to the danger that would threaten Northern Europe if Russia managed to occupy the Sound and turn the Baltic into a Russian lake or if it could obtain a naval port on the west coast of Norway, which easily could be turned into a new Sevastopol some 100 [Swedish, ie., of ten kilometres each] miles from the coast of Scotland. One mustn't ignore the influence of the Press on the so-called public opinion and its influence on governments."[cclxxxviii] And again, on 20th August 1855 "Through my conversations with numerous outstanding and well respected men here, I have managed to draw attention to the importance and threatened situation of the Finnmark."[cclxxxix]

This goes directly to the heart of the issue of whether the King was serious in his negotiations with the Allies. If his intentions were only to fend off unwelcome pressure for Sweden to join a war, there would have been absolutely no need to bring up the Finnmark issue. The 1855 Baltic Campaign had been more subdued than its predecessor; the French senior partner in the Alliance against Russia was already looking to end the war. All the King had to do was nothing. The Allied fleets would eventually sail home and until they could reappear in the Baltic another six months would have passed, when anything could have happened. The fact that the King instead introduced a new issue, whose only effect could be to increase at least British anxiety about the Northern Theatre, strongly supports the view that this was a pretext, aimed at rekindling British interest in a Swedish alliance. This is also the view taken by both Palmstierna and Eriksson.[ccxc]

Could there be another explanation? One possibility is that the King worried that Russia did have plans on the Finnmark; that following a setback in the south, Russia would now turn to the north and that the only way to stop this was to get a guarantee from Russia's enemies. But if this is the case, it begs the question why the issue was not raised in 1854. Moreover, it assumes that Russia really had aggressive designs on Varangerfiord or on the port of Hammerfest and that this was clear to Sweden. Was this the case? Russian sources, needless to say, disagree. Alexander Genrikhovich Jomini, a Russian diplomat who in 1878 wrote a semi-official diplomatic history of the Crimean War (*Étude diplomatique sur la Guerre de Crimée, par Un Ancien Diplomat*) disclaims any Russian territorial ambitions in the north.[ccxci] So too did the Emperor Alexander II, whom Cullberg quotes as exclaiming: "My God! This [the November Treaty] was absolutely unnecessary. The idea of taking one village that belonged to another never entered into my soul."[ccxcii] Cullberg also quotes an unnamed Russian diplomat saying: "We were assigned the idea of making Hammerfest, through a series of fortifications, into a second Sevastopol --- These absurdities would be hardly credible, had they not received the sanction of a formal treaty."[ccxciii]

Palmstierna also feels that there was no ground for believing that Russia intended to seize any territory. But he feels that Russia also handled the earlier negotiations badly. Nevertheless, it was in King Oscar's interest to present the Finnmark question in as threatening a light as possible. In fact, he notes, Russia had plenty of ice-free ports and fiords if necessary – although the Scandinavian (and more importantly, the British) authorities probably did not know this.[ccxciv] Eriksson agrees and notes that Count Frölich, as well as the British and French Ministers Grey and Lobstein, all assumed that the King wanted to be pressured by the Allies and that the Finnmark issue provided the pretext.[ccxcv]

If this was indeed the King intention, it certainly worked. On 10th July, he received the British Minister Magenis in an audience at Haga Palace. The next day, Magenis reported back to Lord Clarendon that he had presented the treaty proposals to the King.[ccxcvi] According to Magenis, King Oscar had said that he always been desirous of intimate relations and an alliance with Great Britain; and also, that if Russia's ambitions were checked in the south, she would try to obtain compensation for that check in the north. According to Cullberg, Magenis had expressed British concerns about Varangerfiord and said that if the King would commit himself to not allow Russian penetration into the Finnmark, Her Majesty's Government would be prepared to conclude a treaty that would guarantee British military and naval support if Russia violated the relevant territory.[ccxcvii] The next day the King received the French Minister Lobstein, who repeated the same message on behalf of his government.[ccxcviii]

There is one mystery here. The proposed treaty must have been discussed within and between the British and French Governments. Yet at least on the British side, there seems to be no record of any discussion preceding Magenis' approach. The closest we get is Jonasson, who writes that Lord Palmerston on 3rd June 1855 read a detailed report on the Finnmark problem, and, believing the issue to be urgent, proposed an agreement with the King of Sweden.[ccxcix] Eriksson gives more details, noting that on 23rd May, 1855, Consul Crowe wrote a report to Lord Clarendon about the Finnmark issue, stating that the Russian demands had been debated at length in the Norwegian Parliament (the Storting) in 1854.[ccc] Crowe's report was accompanied by his longer paper from 1836, *A brief historical Account of Finnmark, and the Rise, Progress, and present State of the Dispute between Norway and Russia, with respect to the Boundary Question and pretended Rights of Russia*.[ccci] Upon reading these reports, Lord Palmerston is supposed to have stated that: "It might be well to enter into some agreement with the King of Sweden and Norway, binding him to make no concession whatever to Russia, whether of Fishery Rights, Pasture Rights or Territory without the consent of Great Britain. Such a Treaty would be a security to us and definite support to him."[cccii] There is further support for this view in a dispatch from Baron Hochschild, the Swedish Minister to the Court of St James. On 4th June 1855, Hochschild reports that he met Lord Palmerston at a ball and had a long conversation with him, where the latter asked him in detail about the Åland Islands. However, the dispatch does not mention any interest in the Finnmark.[ccciii] During this conversation, Hochschild also suggested that if the Åland Islands could not be given to Sweden, they should be neutralised.[cccive]

The first mention of the proposed treaty in British sources other than Foreign Office dispatches seems to be when Lord Clarendon proposed it to the Cabinet on 13th August.[cccv] But at this stage the scope of the treaty had already widened.

The Allied approach had specifically referred to any Russian designs on the Finnmark and Varangerfiord. However, five days after his first report, Magenis wrote to Clarendon that the King wanted the Allied guarantee to be extended to cover the entire territory of the United Kingdoms. Magenis felt that this was because for King Oscar, Sweden was more important than Norway.[cccvi] By contrast, Palmstierna claims that the King was motivated by continued fears of Russian designs on the island of Gotland in the Baltic.[cccvii]

At least one interested party was dubious about the whole idea. In a letter dated 27th July, Queen Victoria wrote to Lord Clarendon, expressing surprise that having denied a guarantee to Sweden when she was on the verge of joining the war (ie., in 1854) because it was deemed too onerous to the Great Britain, the same guarantee was now supposed to be extended without Sweden joining the war.[cccviii] However, the Royal doubts were ignored. On 14th August Magenis wrote to Clarendon that Lobstein had been instructed by the French Government that the King's desire for the guarantee to cover all his territories had been accepted and that the British Government concurred with the French.[cccix]

On the Swedish side, meanwhile, Baron Stierneld had felt uneasy about accepting a guarantee from two warring powers, clearly aimed at inciting Sweden against their enemy. He had therefore telegraphed Manderström in Vienna on 15th July with his doubts, but the latter had reassured him that a defensive treaty was not a hostile act and must be allowed an independent state.[cccx]

Following these initial contacts, there seems to have been a pause. In the meantime, there had been renewed contacts between the Swedish and French Courts. Baroness Bonde had already in June let the Swedish Court know that the French Emperor desired the Swedish Order of the Seraphim.[cccxi] In October, Admiral Virgin, the former Swedish Minister to Britain, travelled to France to invest the Emperor with this decoration. The King's confidential instructions to Virgin reiterated that as long as war was about the Eastern Question and Oriental in scope, the United Kingdoms would maintain their neutrality. "Néanmoins l'Amiral assurera le Comte Walewski des sentiments personels du Roi, et de la satisfaction qu'eproverait S.M. de resserrer encore l'alliance que l'unit déja avec les puissances occidentales et même de joindre ses efforts avec leurs, si la lute actuelle prenait des dimensions de nature à favoriser et assurer l'avenir de Royaumes unis." ("Even so, the Admiral should assure Count Walewski of the King's personal feelings, of his lively sympathy for the noble and just cause of the Allies, and of the satisfaction it would give HM to reaffirm again the alliance which unites him with the western powers and even join his efforts to theirs, if the current struggle took on the nature and dimension that would promote and ensure the future of the United Kingdoms.")[cccxii]

Virgin's mission was reciprocated by a visit to Stockholm by General Canrobert, the victor at Sevastopol, who set off in late October to invest the King and Crown Prince Karl with the Legion d'Honneur. In a letter to the King dated 27th October, the Emperor Napoleon wrote that General Canrobert "possède tout ma confidence et il pourra repondre à toutes les questions que V.M. voudra lui addresser." ("has my complete confidence and he will be able to answer all the questions that Y.M. would care to put to him.")[cccxiii] This visit is important for two reasons. First, because one of the misconceptions at the time – and even later – was that it was Canrobert's visit that had led to the November Treaty.[cccxiv] Canrobert himself was happy to give this impression, eg., by claiming that the November Treaty was signed two days *before* he left, instead of two days *after*.[cccxv]

As is clear from the course of events outlined here, this is wrong. However, the Canrobert visit is also important because the King's detailed discussions with the French General again confirm how serious he was in his desire to join the war.

Canrobert arrived in Stockholm on 6th November and returned to Paris on the 19th. Posthumus describes a very high-profile visit, with a very public and immediate audience with the King on 7th November; a dinner at the Palace; how thousands of citizens gathered in the streets to cheer "The Victor of Inkerman"; and how, at a performance of the Magic Flute on 12th November, the guest was greeted by repeated shouts of "Long live Canrobert, long live France" and the orchestra playing "Partant pour la Syrie", the unofficial French national anthem.[cccxvi] But while the public display was important, the key events were Canrobert's conversations with King Oscar. At the first audience, Canrobert laid out his Emperor's views, which were written down by the King in his diary.[cccxvii] If peace could be concluded over the winter on honourable terms that would safeguard the future, Napoleon felt that it was his duty not to prolong a war that had demanded such great sacrifices in both men and money. However, Russia's stiff-necked attitude gave little hope of such an outcome. If the war were to continue into 1856, the Powers had agreed to shift the theatre of war to the North and pursue it more seriously there. The Emperor had said that nothing could be decided there without the cooperation of the United Kingdoms and wanted to know what King Oscar under certain circumstances thought could and ought to be done to break Russia's power in the north. The King reiterated that as long as the war was about the Oriental Question, he felt that he should stick to his neutrality. But if it was moved to the shores of the Baltic and the concerns of the North would be as warmly embraced by the Allies as they had embraced those of the Orient, then it would be unworthy of the King of Sweden to sit indifferent and inactive.

Over the next ten days, the King held repeated long conversations with Canrobert. During these, the two men drew up detailed plans for a northern campaign, featuring Scandinavian, Danish, French and British troops, a landing in Finland or in Estonia and a march on St Petersburg.[cccxviii] (The King's hand-drawn map of the plan appears in appendix 4.) The King notes that he managed to overcome Canrobert's concerns about wintering in Finland, which he felt was almost unavoidable, regardless of which plan was pursued. But of far greater importance is that King Oscar's notes show that he now gave up his insistence on Austrian participation in the war; as well as easing his demand for a guaranteed conquest of Finland. His diary notes from 9th November are clear: Canrobert had stated that, ideally, the Emperor Napoleon wished to make war together with the German governments, but realised that this could not be certain; the Emperor would also be happy to see Finland reunited with Sweden in order to establish a Northern power strong enough to bloc Russia's ambitious progress, although he could give no guarantees. The diary continues: "I suspect Austria, was my reply, but if any decisive progress is to be made, she must openly declare herself or at least take a threatening position in order to keep a substantial share of Russia's forces in Poland and Podolia. I do not require a guarantee of territorial gain, since this will be dependent on the success of the allied weapons. I simply wish to receive a clear certainty that the war once begun will not be concluded before something decisive has been achieved that will safeguard our future."[cccxix] Henceforth, there was no more talk of Austria joining the actual fighting.

This also seems to have been the time when the King drafted the outline of an offensive treaty between France, Great Britain, Austria and the United Kingdoms which will be covered somewhat later.

Before Canrobert arrived, Magenis had already met Stierneld again and informed him that the treaty proposals were approved and what they contained.[cccxx]

On 30th October, King Oscar met with his two Swedish Prime Ministers, Baron Stierneld (Foreign Affairs) and Count Sparre (Justice) as well as the acting Norwegian Prime Minister Hans Christian Petersen, in order to inform them of the proposed Treaty and ask for their opinions. While all three approved of the Treaty, Stierneld suggested softening the affront to Russia by changing the proposed references to "the Russian Emperor" ("L'Empereur de Russie") to "any power" ("une puissance quelconque"). The King instead suggested instead writing "Russia" ("la Russie"). The King also noted that he wanted it to be made clear that any troops sent to aid him would be at the cost of the sending powers.[cccxxi] The next day, the King invited Magenis to dinner and informed him of the proposed changes. In his dispatch to Lord Clarendon, Magenis recommended agreeing to the changes, noting that he knew that the King's Ministers would have preferred no mention of Russia at all.[cccxxii] Twelve days later, 12th November, Magenis reported a further proposed change, clarifying that the second paragraph should read: "Their said Majesties on their part engage to place at the disposal of His Majesty the King of Sweden and Norway sufficient land and sea forces to cooperate with those of His Majesty the King of Sweden and Norway with the view to resist pretentions or aggressions of Russia." (For the entire text of the treaty, see Appendix 1.) Again, Magenis counselled agreeing, since the change was not material.[cccxxiii] At this meeting Stierneld had also proposed a separate and secret annex to the treaty, broadening the scope of the proposed guarantee to cover any Russian hostilities or acts of war against the United Kingdoms (see Appendix 2).[cccxxiv] This proposal was rejected, but again serves to show the seriousness of the Swedish side in the negotiations.

On the Allied side, there were also some concerns. On 1st November, the King told Magenis that he had heard that Lord Clarendon was concerned about possible parliamentary opposition to the Treaty. He recommended pointing out that the Treaty caused Sweden and Norway to approach the western powers, and that it obviously would have an important influence on his decision if these powers were to decide to break Russia's power in the Baltic as they had successfully done in the Black Sea.[cccxxv] Meanwhile, the French government had expressed concerns that the draft Treaty was too defensive. To this Lord Palmerston replied in a letter to Clarendon on 25th September 1855, that the Swedish treaty would be "the attainment by anticipation of part of the objectives of the war." It would check Russian expansion in the north, and prevent Sweden from acting against the interests of the Allies. "The Treaty we propose would be a *part of a long line of circumvallation* to confine the future expansion of Russia even if the events of the war should not enable us to drive her outposts in at any part of her present circumference."[cccxxvi]

These concerns were clearly not significant enough to derail the process, because on 21st November, the treaty was signed in Stockholm by Stierneld, Magenis and Lobstein. On 28th November it was ratified in Windsor, a day later in Paris and the day after that in Stockholm.[cccxxvii]

As noted above, the coincidence of Canrobert's visit with the signing of the November Treaty led to the view that one led to the other. As has been made clear, this was not the case. A second point frequently made is that the November Treaty contained secret clauses that would transform it into an offensive treaty. Greenhill and Giffard give no reference, but simply write that "Further secret clauses provided for a joint military action in Finland."[cccxxviii] Mosse claims that the November Treaty was accompanied by an exchange of notes establishing the conditions in which it was to be converted into an offensive alliance against Russia, a point repeated by Jonasson (see above, p. 6).[cccxxix] Nordin reported that "everyone" – in this case meaning in the Russian capital – assumed that there were secret clauses to the Treaty.[cccxxx] Lambert repeats the Russian view, but notes that it is unlikely, since if there had been such clauses, there would have been no need to discuss an offensive treaty, yet this was in fact being discussed.[cccxxxi]

There is a further indication that there were no secret clauses to the November Treaty. Sometime in November, probably during Canrobert's visit (the word "Canrobert" is written on the draft, but the word is not in the King's handwriting, so this is not absolutely certain), the King drew up in his own hand a draft offensive treaty.[cccxxxii] This draft, which does not seem to have been published anywhere, appears in Appendix 3, in the original French and translated into English. In summary, the draft sets out a treaty between France, Britain, Austria and Sweden & Norway, the aim of which is to limit Russian power in Northern Europe. In furtherance of this aim, France, Britain and Sweden & Norway will make joint war on Russia, with the Swedish contribution subsidised by the French and British governments. The King of Sweden & Norway will have supreme command in the Northern theatre. There will be no separate peace with Russia. Finally, the treaty parties will invite Denmark to join the treaty and take part in the war. Denmark will also receive subsidies. But the Danish government will also receive a guarantee for the integrity of the Danish monarchy as defined by the London Protocol of 1852. The last clause opens up an interesting perspective. Had this treaty been signed and had Denmark joined on such terms, then, when in 1864 Prussia went to war with Denmark over the Schleswig-Holstein question, it would have faced the armed opposition not only of Denmark, but of Austria, France, Great Britain and the United Kingdoms. It is fascinating – although ultimately meaningless – to speculate in what this would have meant for the future of Europe.

Regardless of the existence or not of secret clauses to the November Treaty, it was clearly seen by contemporaries as paving the way for Swedish participation in the war – beginning with King Oscar himself, who indicated to Crowe that the November Treaty had fulfilled his conditions and that if the war continued in 1856, Sweden/Norway would see it necessary to take part. The second act of the drama would probably be played out in the Baltic. In this phase, the question of the role of the United Kingdoms would again come to the fore "and the solution --- was not difficult to arrive at."[cccxxxiii]

Foreign observers were equally clear about their thoughts. Prince Metternich, when asked, "Le traité conclu a Stockholm, est-il défensif et offensif contre la Russie?" replied "Non, il est défensif et offensant." ("Is the treaty concluded in Stockholm defensive or offensive towards Russia? No, it is defensive and offending.")[cccxxxiv] But the key reaction was that of Russia. When informing the Russian government of the Treaty, General de Nordin had been instructed to speak plainly and amply. He was to express Swedish concerns that, if checked in the south, Russia would turn towards the Baltic; and that to rely on Russia's good will was to ignore the lessons of history and Sweden's sad memories. In fact, the drafted note was so harsh that de Nordin was told not to hand it to Nesselrode but instead deliver a more diplomatically formulated one.[cccxxxv] Even so, the news of the Treaty seems to have come as a shock to the Russian government. The Russian Minister in Stockholm had not been aware of the negotiations and so had not warned his government. Nordin reports that when Nesselrode was told of the treaty, he exclaimed "Comment! Il y a un Traité?" ("What! There is a Treaty?")[cccxxxvi] The reaction of the new Emperor Alexander II has already been mentioned (see p. 77). Nesselrode also pointed out that the question of the Finnmark had been given much greater importance by the Swedish government than it deserved. He conceded that a treaty might have been justified when the war broke out; but that there had been no events during the two years of war that could justify it in 1855. The only motivation therefore had to be that the Western Powers were attempting to raise new enemies against Russia.[cccxxxvii]

The Swedish side now tried to muddy the waters. The King told the Danish Minister to Stockholm, Count Scheel-Plessen, that he had been approached by the Western Powers and that duty bound him to accept their proffered guarantee.[cccxxxviii] Meanwhile, Stierneld told Dashkov that the king had been forced to act by Western pressure and by Swedish public opinion.[cccxxxix] None of this seems to have had much impact.

The Danish Foreign Minister von Scheele captured a general feeling when he wrote to Scheel-Plessen noting that it was highly unlikely that Russia, at a time when half of Europe was in arms against, it would really attempt to add another enemy to the list.[cccxl]

But if King Oscar and most contemporaries saw the November Treaty as the precursor of Swedish participation in the war, was this also the intention of the Allies? This is not quite as clear. If the war had continued in 1856, the Allies were planning an assault in the North.[cccxli] In that case, Sweden's participation was both desirable and welcome. But there is also a strong argument that the Treaty was intended to put pressure on Russia to accept the latest Allied and Austrian ultimatum for negotiations. Hallendorff points out that for the Allies, the point of offering a territorial guarantee on account of Varangerfiord was to lure the United Kingdoms into a treaty which by its generous nature could not well be rejected, but which expressed their distrust of Russia and sent a clear sign to Russia about changing Swedish attitudes. In turn, this should strengthen peace feeling in St Petersburg; and if not, draw Sweden closer to the Allies.[cccxlii]

However, in Sweden, the King seemed convinced that Sweden's entry into the war was now around the corner. On 16th January 1856, he received his friend General Löwenhielm and discussed with him the plans for an offensive treaty and for the war in 1856, assuming that the war would continue. When the practical Löwenhielm asked about the cost, the King replied "This is too big a subject to talk about, but be confident when I sum up by telling you that everything has been dealt with; the sums we previously spoke about have been completely accepted and once the offensive treaty is signed I can present the first draft for cash."[cccxliii] The next day the King received a telegram from de Nordin in St Petersburg: "Russia accepts *purement et simplement* the through Austria presented conditions."[cccxliv] The news came as a shock.[cccxlv] Several contemporary observers report that the King was deeply shaken by the news. Crown Prince Karl asked the Marshal of the Court if he did not agree that the King had aged ten years since the morning.[cccxlvi]

Throughout the winter of 1855/56, the Allies had discussed plans for the coming year. In early January, a great Council of War was held in the Tuileries Palace in Paris, chaired by the Emperor Napoleon, while a parallel one, chaired by Vaillant, the Minister of War, discussed plans for the Baltic.[cccxlvii] On the Russian side, there were similar discussions. On 28th December 1855, an Austrian envoy delivered an ultimatum. Unless Russia agreed to peace on the basis of the Four (actually Five) Points, Austria would declare war. The ultimatum was set to expire on 18th January 1856. To discuss the reply, the Russian Emperor called two Crown Councils, on 1st and 15th January. The Crown Councils were dominated by the likelihood that if the war continued, hitherto neutral powers – mainly Austria and Sweden – actively would join Russia's enemies, warnings repeatedly made by Nesselrode, as well as by other Ministers.[cccxlviii] The Emperor was told that Russia lacked the capacity to fight all these enemies.[cccxlix] At the second Crown Council, it was agreed to accept the Austrian ultimatum. (An interesting question is whether Austria really would have declared war. Its behaviour throughout the conflict was aimed at avoiding war. However, the main point here is that Russia clearly believed that Austria was ready to go to war.)

Could the November Treaty, if concluded earlier, have hastened the end of the war? This is obviously one of those "what if" questions that are impossible to answer. However, regardless of whether the answer is yes or no, there is a case to be made that the November Treaty would not have been concluded earlier. The point has been repeatedly made (eg, p. 41) that the Allies lacked the capacity to fight a two-front land war. Once the Crimea had become the main theatre, they could not, therefore, realistically open another front in the north. Moreover, they could reasonably expect that, once they had taken Sevastopol, Russia would make peace. Meanwhile, for Russia, making peace as long as Sevastopol held out, was not on the cards. But if Russia insisted on continuing the war once

Sevastopol had fallen, the Allies had a problem. Continuing the war in the south was unlikely to lead to any decisive result. On the other hand, with the Crimean Campaign over, there were troops available to move to another theatre. This opened a window of opportunity for a treaty with Sweden. If the treaty caused Russia to give up the fight – as the Emperor Napoleon seems to have hoped – then well and good. If it did not – apparently Lord Palmerston's preferred option – then the war would have to shift to the only place where the Allies could fight Russia, namely the Baltic, in which case a Swedish alliance was certainly welcome and probably necessary.

Although King Oscar was sceptical about Russia's sincerity, this was to all intents and purposes the end of the war. On 15th February the Peace Conference opened in Paris and on 30th March the peace was signed. Over the months of negotiations, King Oscar scrambled to salvage something from the situation. When the peace negotiations started, he attempted to have Sweden represented at the talks, but this was rejected by the Allies, who claimed that they would safeguard Swedish interests.[cccl] He then presented three Swedish demands to the conference:

The limitation of Russian naval power in Baltic and White Seas;

Åland to be ceded to Sweden, or neutralised, either under the protection of the Western Powers or – preferably – Sweden; and

A ban on Russian fortifications on Åland and on the Finnish coast north and west of Sveaborg.[cccli]

However, Russia was – unsurprisingly – loath to cede territory to a country that had not taken part in the war. Nor were the Allied powers prepared to press Russia on Sweden's behalf if this would risk prolonging the war. Ultimately, the only result gained was that the Åland Islands were demilitarised – as they remain to this day. In addition, Sweden had gained greater respect for the right of neutrals; and could claim some of the credit for the outlawing of privateering at the Paris Conference. Finally, Sweden had escaped Russian wardship. In view of Sweden's subsequent neutrality, it is perhaps fitting that the country's last attempt to play a major role in a European war should lead to such non-belligerent results.

Chapter 5: Conclusion

Much of the answer to the research questions has been covered in chapters 3 and 4. This conclusion will restate the research questions and summarise the answers. The chapter shows that both the Allies and the United Kingdoms were serious in their negotiations – but that their desires to have Sweden join in the war never peaked at the same time. Had Sweden joined, the main contribution could have been made by its navy. But even though Sweden never did take part in the war, the negotiations between the two sides and the November Treaty did contribute to bringing the war to an end.

The first research question was whether the negotiations were serious – on both sides. The thesis argues that the answer to this question is yes. Even before the war, the Allies had counted on Swedish participation. During and after the 1854 Baltic Campaign, there were repeated attempts to entice Sweden into the war, eg, by offering the Åland Islands. By 1855, the Allies knew that they could project overwhelming naval power in the Baltic without Swedish participation. Moreover, a possible aim – diverting Russian resources to the North and away from the Crimea – was already achieved, again without Sweden going to war. Yet the negotiations continued and eventually led to the November Treaty. The Treaty was a guarantee to go to war on Sweden's and Norway's behalf. While there is an argument that the Allied aim was to play on Russia's fear of more enemies, they could not be certain that this would work. Moreover, following the fall of Sevastopol, the Allies were in a quandary. Unless Russia agreed to make peace, they would have to continue the war. Doing so in the south would be difficult and unlikely to have much effect. By contrast, attacking Russia in the Baltic, threatening St Petersburg, could force the war to a successful conclusion. Here, the participation of the United Kingdoms could be useful.

On the Swedish side, the answer is equally yes. King Oscar had proclaimed the neutrality of his realms and had this accepted by all parties. If he had not been interested in taking a step further and joining the war, he need not have engaged in the negotiations with the Allies. Even without the King's diary notes, which clearly show his desire to take part in the war – albeit on his conditions – this shows that he too was serious.

However, it could be claimed that the King played an "Austrian" game, in other words, that he pretended eagerness but in fact set a price that he knew the Allies were never going to meet. This is possible – but also unlikely. His diary notes argue against this interpretation, as does the fact that when the Allies seemed less keen, he changed from courted to suitor and lowered the price for Swedish participation in the war. The draft offensive treaty described on page 86 further argues against this view. Why draw up an offensive treaty which – seemingly – was never presented to the putative allies, if the aim was not to go to war?

The second research question was whether Sweden could realistically have taken part in the war. Sweden had a large army relative to its population. But the army was unprepared for war, and, more importantly, unwilling to fight. Already in 1854, officers had expressed their opposition to joining the war in the press. During that year, officer resignations doubled, both because officers still adhered to the 'Policy of 1812' and because they worried that the army was in no shape to fight. The more senior in rank, the more opposed the officers tended to be.[ccclii] Financially, Sweden would have needed, and throughout the negotiations insisted upon, substantial subsidies – 5 million francs (£200,000) per month. Although King Oscar did stress to his Allied interlocutors that this still made the Swedish participation cost-effective,[cccliii] Swedish opponents of the war noted that Sardinia joined without receiving any subsidies.[cccliv]

The next research question – what could Sweden have contributed to the war – is related to the previous one. Here, the answer is less clear-cut. The operations in the Baltic certainly showed that in 1854 and – perhaps to a lesser extent

– in 1855, the Swedish navy, with its 200 gunboats of different sizes, could have been useful. Had the war continued in 1856, the same is likely to be true. Using Swedish territory as a base for an attack on Russia would no doubt have been useful, but the success of the Allies in landing in the Crimea shows that it might not be strictly necessary. (The comparison is not entirely apt. In Crimea, the French and British were within easy distance of their ally Turkey. Moreover, bad as the Black Sea climate could be, the Northern winters were a traumatic memory for the French, who in their negotiations with Sweden were distinctly uncomfortable merely at the thought of having to spend the cold season on Åland.[ccclv]) As for the Swedish army, its size might have made it useful, but its quality and willingness to fight (see above) was doubtful. However, as discussed under the first research question, the threat of Swedish participation in the war could, and in fact did, have an effect on Russia's willingness to make peace. As Jonasson (and others) point out, it is ironic that the November Treaty, which was supposed to pave the way for Sweden to go to war, instead helped ensure that this would not happen.[ccclvi] This raises a supplementary question: would an earlier treaty have had the same effect? This is difficult to judge, but it is likely that it was the timing of the November Treaty – following the fall of Sevastopol, with uncertainty about where the war would now continue – that made it so effective. This is further elaborated below.

Finally, why was it that the protracted negotiations, at one point or other actively pursued by Britain, by France and by the King of Sweden & Norway, never led to Swedish participation in the war? There are a number of answers. One is that the Allies were never able or willing to fulfil two of Sweden's conditions, Austrian participation in the war and the Swedish reconquest of Finland. A more important reason seems to be that the respective parties' ardour for an agreement never peaked at the same time. In 1854, the French were the keenest on a Swedish alliance. Some members of the British government were interested, but when the question was put to the Cabinet, the idea was rejected. As for Sweden, the

King felt that, being the approached party, he could hold out for all his conditions to be fulfilled. In addition, the lacklustre performance of the Allied fleets in the 1854 Baltic Campaign tended to dampen the Swedish ardour for going to war.

By contrast, in 1855, the French government was less interested, with Napoleon III already contemplating how to end the war. The new British government under Lord Palmerston was more eager, but Britain lacked the capacity to fight a two-front war alone. The perceived Allied coolness led to a corresponding rise in Swedish eagerness, eventually making King Oscar moderate his demands for an alliance.

There was also another factor. As long as the focus of the war was in the Crimea, the Allies had less interest in a Swedish alliance. They presumably hoped that, once Sevastopol had fallen, Russia would consent to make peace. But, as long as Sevastopol held out, Russia had little reason to give up the fight. The problem for the Allies became acute when Sevastopol fell and Russia still showed little inclination to make peace. Either they had to make peace on unsatisfactory terms; or else continue the war elsewhere. This confluence of factors – moderation of the Swedish demands, the Allied need to press matters – opened a window of opportunity when both sides' eagerness for agreement peaked at the same time, and allowed the negotiations leading up to the November Treaty to be successfully concluded.

Of course, the ultimate reason why Sweden never joined in the war was that the war ended. Had the war continued in 1856, the evidence is overwhelming that Sweden would have joined the Franco-British alliance as a belligerent.

Acknowledgements

In 2014, Sweden will celebrate 200 years of unbroken neutrality. But although this is sometimes seen as the result of a skilful and consistent policy by successive Swedish governments, an arguably greater role has been played by luck, and by circumstances. Nor has neutrality always been the avowed goal of the Swedish establishment. In the Crimean War, we find the King of Sweden and Norway actively pursuing a policy aimed at participation in the war against Russia; while his government and army were still dominated by those who believed that Sweden should be Russia's friend, or at least not her enemy.

While the Crimean War has been treated in detail by numerous non-Swedish historians, it is today, perhaps, one of the less remembered wars of British history. The Baltic campaign is remembered even less and the negotiations with Sweden possibly least of all. What is related, is not infrequently wrong. Swedish language coverage has been greater, but not for the last 60 or so years. The increased Swedish interest in history since the mid-1980s has not yet filled this gap. This thesis is an attempt to cast light on what was perhaps Sweden's last attempt to play a major military role.

A number of people have been instrumental in the production of the thesis. My tutor, Professor Saul David at the University of Buckingham, suggested a 19th Century theme. He has patiently read and reread the successive drafts and provided invaluable suggestions, comments and assistance. There will still be mistakes – they are all my own.

My thanks are also due to the staff at The National Archives in Kew, the British Library and the London Library; as well as to Kungliga Biblioteket (the National Library of Sweden) and Riksarkivet (the National Archive of Sweden).

I am grateful to H.M. King Carl XVI Gustaf of Sweden for graciously granting me permission to study his great-great-great grandfather's personal papers. My very special thanks are also due to Ingemar Carlsson and Arvid Jakobsson of the Bernadotte Family Archive, who provided me not only with material from the archives and chaperoned me during my research sessions in the Royal Palace in Stockholm; but who also provided guidance and suggestions for further reading.

My wife Fiona, who one day brought home a leaflet from a bookshop informing me of the MA course, and who has put up with a husband whose idea of Saturday relaxation is to go off to spend the day reading 19th Century correspondence at The National Archives and then having to listen to him talking about it, deserves more thanks than can be expressed. My daughter Zoë thinks I am mad and may well be right, but she puts up with me anyway.

London, 2010
Gabriel Stein

Bibliography
A: Primary sources, unpublished
(i) Official documents
(a) National Archive, London (TNA)
Foreign Office correspondence
Foreign Office and predecessor: Political and Other Departments: General Correspondence before 1906, Sweden (later incorporating Norway), (FO 73)
Vol 254
Vol 255
Vol 259
Vol 260
Vol 261
Vol 262
Vol 263
Vol 266
Vol 269
Vol 270
Vol 271

Foreign Office From the Captain of the Baltic Fleet 1854 (FO 634/3)
Foreign Office Confidential Print Crowe Report (FO 881/494)
Foreign Office Confidential Print November Treaty (FO 881/714)
Home Office War: Rear Admiral Sir John Ross, on hostilities in Baltic (HO 45/5875)
Admiralty Letter Book of Admiral Sir Chas. Napier during Baltic Campaign (ADM 7/769)
Maps and plans
Foreign Office General chart of the Baltic or East Sea (FO 925/3508)
War Office Plans and maps relating to the Crimean War (WO 78)
1028

1031

(b) Riksarkivet (National Archives of Sweden, Stockholm, RA)
Utrikesdepartementet (Foreign Office) (UD)
UDs huvudarkiv (Foreign Office main archive) (UD HA)
Statsrådsprotokoll i utrikesdepartementsärenden (Cabinet minutes, Foreign Office issues) 1853-1854 (A3A)
Vol 6
Vol 7
Utrikesdepartementet 1902 års dossiersystem (Foreign Office, 1902 filing system)
1 O Novembertraktaten (The November Treaty)
Vol 48
Vol 49
21 F Krimkriget (The Crimean War)
Vol 1104
Vol 1105
Vol 1106
92 T Byteshandeln mellan Finland och Archangelsk under Krimkriget (The trade between the Finnmark and Arkhangelsk during the Crimean War)
Vol 4494

(ii) Private papers

(a) National Archive, London (TNA)
Lord John Russell, Minutes & memoranda (FO 96-24)
Lord John Russell Papers: Correspondence and Papers (PRO 32/22/11D)
2nd Earl Granville, Confidential Print, (PRO 30/29/255)

(b) Bernadotte Family Archive, Stockholm (BFA)
Personal papers of King Oscar I & Queen Josefina (O1 & J)
Vol 36
Vol 37
Vol 47
Vol 48
Personal papers of Crown Prince Karl, later King Karl XV (KXV)
Vol 14

Vol 15
Personal Papers of Prince Oscar, Duke of Östergötland, later King Oscar II (OII)
Vol 118

B: Primary Sources, published

(i) Contemporary Publications

An Amateur, *How about Cronstadt? Reflections upon a trip to the Baltic Fleet, with a few Remarks on the progress and prosecution of the War with Russia under the present administration*, London, 1855 (JSTOR)

A G Jomini, *Étude diplomatique sur la Guerre de Crimée, par Un Ancien Diplomat*, St Petersburg, 1878

(ii) Published letters and memoirs

Benson & Esher (eds), *The Letters of Queen Victoria: A Selection of Her Majesty's Correspondence between the Years 1836 and 1861, volumes II & III*, London 1908

The Hon Evelyn Ashley, MP, *The Life and Correspondence of Henry John Temple, Viscount Palmerston, vol II*, London 1879

D Bonner-Smith & Captain Alfred Charles Dewar (eds), *Russian War, 1854, Baltic and Black Sea: official correspondence*, London 1943

D Bonner-Smith (ed), *Russian War, 1855, Baltic: official correspondence*, London 1944

B Earp (ed) *The History of the Baltic Campaign of 1854. From documents and other materials furnished by Vice-Admiral Sir Charles Napier*. London 1857

Carl Hallendorff, *Oscar I, Napoleon och Nikolaus – ur diplomaternas privata brev under Krimkriget, (Oscar I, Napoleon and Nikolaus – from the diplomats' private letters during the Crimean War)*, Stockholm, 1918

The Right Hon Sir Herbert Maxwell, *The Life and Letters of George William Frederick Fourth Earl of Clarendon, KG, GCB*, London 1913

Elers Napier, The *Life and Correspondence of Admiral Sir Charles Napier, K.C.B, volume II* London 1862

Charles Stuart Parker, *Life and letters of Sir James Graham, Second Baronet of Netherby*, London 1907

Posthumus (Johan Carl Hellberg), *Ur minnet och dagboken om Mina Samtida, Personer och Händelser efter 1815 inom och utom Fäderneslandet, (From my memory and diary on contemporary persons and events after 1815 within and without the fatherland), Parts VII and VIII*, Stockholm, 1871

Hugh Noel Williams, *The Life and letters of Admiral Sir Charles Napier K.C.B.*, London 1917

(iii) Newspapers

Daily News
Göteborgs Handels- och Sjöfartstidning
Helsingfors Morgonbladet
Indépendence Belge
Post och Inrikes Tidningar
The Times
Wiborg

C: Secondary Sources

(i) Articles and Chapters

Edgar Anderson, The Crimean War in the Baltic Area, *Journal of Baltic Studies*, 5:4 339-361

Edgar Anderson, The Scandinavian Area and the Crimean War in the Baltic, *Scandinavian Studies, 41* (August 1969), 263-275

C I Hamilton, Sir James Graham, the Baltic Campaign and War-Planning at the Admiralty in 1854, *The Historical Journal, 19*, Cambridge, 1976, p 89-112 (JSTOR)

Axel E Jonasson, The Crimean War, the Beginning of Strict Swedish Neutrality and the Myth of Swedish Intervention in the Baltic, *Journal of Baltic Studies 4,* 1973, pp. 244-53

W E Mosse, How Russia Made Peace September 1855 to April 1856, Cambridge Historical Journal, 11-3, 1955, pp. 297-316

T E Toomey, Victoria Cross 1854-1889 and how won, London,1889 (JSTOR)

(ii) Books (including published theses)

Winfried Baumgart, *The Crimean War 1853-1856*, London, 2000

Winston Spencer Churchill, *A History of the English Speaking Peoples, Volume IV The Great Democracies*, London, 1958

John Campbell, Marquis of Lorne, *Viscount Palmerston KG*, London 1892

J B Conacher, *The Aberdeen Coalition 1852-1855, A study in mid-nineteenth century party politics*, Cambridge, 1968

J B Conacher, *Britain and the Crimea: Problems of War and Peace*, London 1987

Albin Cullberg *La politique du roi Oscar I pendant la guerre de Crimée : études diplomatiques sur les négociations secrètes entre les cabinets de Stockholm, Paris, Saint Pétersbourg et Londres les années 1853-1856*, Stockholm 1912

John Shelton Curtiss, *Russia's Crimean War*, Durham, North Carolina, 1979

Saul David, *Victoria's Wars*, London, 2007

Sven Eriksson, *Svensk diplomati och tidningspress under Krimkriget (Swedish diplomacy and newspapers during the Crimean War)*, Stockholm, 1939 (academic dissertation)

George MacDonald Fraser, *Flashman at the Charge*, London, 1974

Basil Greenhill & Ann Giffard, *The British Assault on Finland 1854-1844 – A Forgotten Naval War*, London, 1988

Carl Hallendorff, *Konung Oscar I:s politik under Krimkriget (The policy of King Oscar I during the Crimean War)*, Uppsala, 1930 (Lecture given on the occasion of his accession to the Royal Swedish Academy of Letters, History and Antiquities, 3rd November 1922; includes substantial primary material)

Allan Jansson, *Försvarsfrågan i svensk politik, från 1809 till Krimkriget (The defence question in Swedish politics from 1809 to the Crimean War)*, Uppsala, 1935 (academic dissertation)

Alexander William Kinglake, *The Invasion of the Crimea:*

Its origin and an account of its progress down to the death of Lord Raglan, Third edition, London, 1863, vol I

Andrew D Lambert, *The Crimean War: British Grand Strategy 1853-1856*, Manchester 1991

Herman Lindkvist, *Historien om Sverige, Ånga och Dynamit (Swedish History, Volume VIII, Steam and Dynamite)*, Stockholm, 1999

W E Mosse, *The rise and fall of the Crimean System 1855-71*, London, 1963

C F Palmstierna, *Sverige, Ryssland och England 1833-1855 – Kring novembertraktatens förutsättningar, (Sweden, Russia and England 1833-1855, On the background to the November Treaty)*, PhD thesis, Stockholm 1932

Trevor Royle, *Crimea – The Great Crimean War*, London, 1999

Carl Michael Runeberg, *Sveriges politik under Krimkriget, Neutralitetsförklaringen 1853-1854, (Swedish policy during the Crimean War, the Declaration of Neutrality 1853-1854)*, PhD thesis, Ekenäs, Finland, 1934

Carl Michael Runeberg, *Finland under Orientaliska Kriget (Finland during the Oriental War)*, Helsingfors, 1962

W C Sellar & R J Yeatman, *1066 and All That*, London 2005

F A Simpson, *Louis Napoleon and the Recovery of France 1848-1856*, London 1923

Eva Helen Ulvros, *Oscar I – En biografi, (Oscar I, a Biography)*, Lund, 2007

David Wetzel, *The Crimean War: A Diplomatic History*, New York, 1985

Appendices

Appendix 1 – The November Treaty[ccclvii]

SA Majesté la Reine du Royaume Uni de la Grande Bretagne et d'Irlande, Sa Majesté l'Empereur de Français, et Sa Majesté le Roi de Suède et de Norvége, désirant prévenir toute complicacion de nature à troubler l'equilibre Européen, ont résolut de s'entendre dans le but d'assurer l'intégrité des Royaumes Unis de Suède et de Norvége, et ont nommé Plénipotentiaires pour conclur un Traité a cet effet, savoir:

Sa Majesté la Reine du Royaume Uni de la Grande Bretagne et d'Irlande, le Sieur Arthur Charles Magenis, Ecuyer, Son Envoyé Extraordinaire et Ministre Plénipotentiaire près Sa Majesté le Roi de Suède et de Norvége;

Sa Majesté l'Empereur de Français, le Sieur Charles Victor Lobstein, Officier de l'Ordre Impérial de la Légion d'Honneur, Grande-Croix de l'Ordre Royal de l'Etoile Polaire de Suède, Commandeur de l'Ordre du Christ et Chevalier de selui de la Conception de Portugal, Son Envoyé Extraordinaire et Ministre Plénipotentiaire près Sa Majesté le Roi de Suède et de Norvége;

Et Sa Majesté le Roi de Suède et de Norvége, le Sieur Gustave Nicholas Algernon Adolphe Baron Stierneld, Son Ministre d'Etat et des Affaires Etrangères, Chevalier et Commandeur de Ses Ordres, Grand-Croix de Son Ordre de Saint Olaf de Norvége, &c., &c.;

Lesquels, après s'être communiqué leurs plein pouvoits respectifs, trouvés en bonne et due forme, son convenus de ce qui suit: –

ARTICLE I.

Sa Majesté le Roi de Suède et de Norvége s'engage à ne céder à la Russie, ni à échanger avec elle, ni à lui permettre d'occuper, aucune partie des territoires appartenant aux Couronnes de Suède et de Norvége. Sa Majesté le Roi de Suède et de Norvége s'engage, en outre, à ne céder à la Russie acun droit de pâturage, de pêche, ou de quelque autre nature que soit, tant sur les dits territoires que sur les côtes de Suède et de Norvége, et à repousser toute pretention que pourrait élever la Russie à établir l'existence d'aucun des droits précites.

ARTICLE II

Dans le cas où la Russie ferait a Sa Majesté le Roi de Suède et de Norvége quelque proposition ou demande ayant pour objet d'obtenir soit la cession ou l'échange d'une partie quelconque des territoires appartenant aux Couronnes de Suède et de Norvége, soit la faculté d'occuper certains points de dit territorire, soit la cession de droit de pêche, de pasturage, ou tout autre sur ces mêmes territories et sur les côtes de Suède et de Norvége, Sa Majesté le Roi de Suède et de Norvége s'engageà communiqué immédiatemment cette proposition ou demande à Sa Majesté la Reine du Royaume Uni de la Grande Bretagne et d'Irlande et à Sa Majesté l'Empereur de Français; et leurs dites Majestés prennent de leur côté, l'engagement de fournir à Sa Majesté le Roi de Suède et de Norvége des force navales et militaries suffisantes pour coopérer avec les forces navales et militaries de Sa dite Majesté, dans le but de resister aux pretentions ou aux aggressions de la Russie. La nature, l'importance, et la destination des forces don't il s'agit, seront, le cas échéant, arrêtes d'un commun accord entre les trois Puissances.

ARTICLE III

Le présent Traité sera ratifié, et es ratifications seront échangées à Stockholm le plus tot que se fairer pourra.

En foi qoui les Plénipotentiaires respectifs l'ont signé, et y ont appose le cachet de leurs armes.

Fait à Stockholm, le vingt-un Novembre, l'an de grace mil huit cent cinquante-cinq.

ARTHUR C. MAGENIS.   V. LOBSTEIN.

[Translation]

HER Majesty the Queen of the United Kingdom of Great Britain and Ireland, His Majesty the Emperor of the French, and His Majesty the King of Sweden and Norway, wishing to prevent any complication likely to disturb the European equilibrium, have resolved to join with the aim of guaranteeing the integrity of the United Kingdoms of Sweden and Norway, and have named Plenipotentiaries to conclude a Treaty to this effect, namely:

Her Majesty the Queen of the United Kingdom of Great Britain and Ireland, Mr Arthur Charles Magenis, Esquire, Her Envoy Extraordinary and Minister Plenipotentiary to His Majesty the King of Sweden and Norway;

His Majesty the Emperor of the French, Mr Charles Victor Lobstein, Officer of the Imperial Order of the Legion of Honour, Grand Cross of the Royal Swedish Order of the North Star, Commander of the Order of Christ and Knight of that of the Conception of Portugal, His Envoy Extraordinary and Minister Plenipotentiary to His Majesty the King of Sweden and Norway;

And His Majesty the King of Sweden and Norway, Mr Gustaf Nicholas Algernon Adolph Baron Stierneld, His Minister of State and of Foreign Affairs, Knight and Commander of His Orders, Grand Cross of His Norwegian Order of St Olaf, &c., &c.;

Who, after having communicated their respective plenipotentiary powers and found these good and in due order, have agreed on the following: –

ARTICLE I.

His Majesty the King of Sweden and Norway undertakes to not cede to Russia, nor to exchange with her, nor allow her to occupy any part of the territories belonging to the Crowns of Sweden and Norway. His Majesty the King of Sweden and Norway further undertakes to not cede to Russia any right of pasturage, of fishing, or of any other kind whatsoever, neither in the said territories nor on the coasts of Sweden and Norway, and to reject any kind of claim that could allow Russia to establish the existence of any of the previously said rights.

ARTICLE II

In case Russia makes any proposal or demand on His Majesty the King of Sweden and Norway, the object of which is to obtain either the cession or the exchange of any part whatsoever of the territories belonging to the Crowns of Sweden and Norway, either the right to occupy certain of the said territories, or the cession of the rights of fishing, of pasturage, or any other of these same territories and on the coasts of Sweden and Norway, His Majesty the King of Sweden and Norway undertakes to immediately communicate this proposal or demand to Her Majesty the Queen of the United Kingdom of Great Britain and Ireland and to His Majesty the Emperor of the French; and their said Majesties, will on their part undertake to provide His Majesty the King of Sweden and Norway naval and military forces sufficient to cooperate with His said Majesty's naval and military forces, with the aim of resisting the Russian claims or aggression. The nature, importance and destination of the forces in question, will, depending on the case, be determined by mutual agreement between the three Powers.

ARTICLE III

The present Treaty will be ratified and the ratifications will be exchanged in Stockholm as soon as can be arranged.

In witness of which the respective Plenipotentiaries have signed it and affixed their seals.

Done in Stockholm, the twenty-first of November, the year of grace eighteen hundred fifty-five.

ARTHUR C. MAGENIS.   V. LOBSTEIN.

Appendix 2 – Secret article proposed by Baron Stierneld[ccclviii]

Article separé et secret

Proposé le 12 Novembre par M ? Stierneld

Dans le ca ou, sans faire a S. M. le Roi de Suède et de Norvége les propositions ou demandes mentionnes dans l'art II du Traité de ce jour, la Russie menaçerait d'hostilités ou se mettrait en état de guerre avec les Royaumes de Suède et de Norvége, S. M. le Roi de Suède et de Norvége s'engage à communiquer immediatement à S.M.l'Empereur de Français et à S.M. Britannique ces dispositions aggressives de la Russie, et leurs dites Majesté s'engagent de leur coté à moins que les dites difficultés au puisses etre aplanies par la voie des négociations, a prêter egalement à S.M. le Roi de Suède et de Norvége les cooperations stipulés par l'art II du Traité de ce jours.

Les forces de terre et de mer des trois haut parties contractant seront a leur charge respective.

Le present article separé et secret aura la même force et valeur que s'il était inséré mot à mot dans le Traité de ce jour et sera ratifié en même temps.

[Translation]

Separate and secret article

Proposed on 12th November [1855] by M Stierneld

In case Russia, without presenting to H.M. the King of Sweden and Norway proposals or demands mentioned in art II of the Treaty dated today, threatens hostilities or enters into a state of war with the Kingdoms of Sweden and Norway, H.M. the King of Sweden and Norway undertakes to communicate immediately to H.M. the Emperor of the French and H.M. the British Queen the Russian aggressive dispositions, and their said Majesties undertake on their part that unless these difficulties are resolved through negotiations, to extend to H.M. the King of Sweden and Norway the same co-operation stipulated in art II of the treaty dated today.

The forces of land and sea of the three high contracting parties shall be at their respective cost.

This separate and secret article shall have the same force and validity as if it were inserted word for word in the Treaty of this day and ratified at the same time.

Appendix 3 – Draft offensive treaty[ccclix]
Articles secret
Article 1er
S.M.l'Empereur d'Autriche, S.M.l'Empereur de Français, S.M.la Reine du Royaume Uni de Grande Bretagne et d'Irlande et S.M. le Roi de Suède et de Norvége, reconaissant l'importance qu'auraient pour l'Europe entière l'affaiblissement de la puissance Russe dans la mer Baltique et le retablissement, autant que les circonstances pourrait le permettre, de l'equilibre politique du Nord compromis par les agrandissements de la Russie, se promettent une alliance intime ainsi que l'union de leurs efforts pour obtenir se resultat.

Article II
S.M.l'Empereur de Français, S.M.la Reine du Royaume Uni de Grande Bretagne et d'Irlande et S.M.le Roi de Suède et de Norvége s'engage à mettre en campagne le printemps prochain, pour le but precedent… homme des troupes de terre et des forces navales suffisant pour dominer la mer Baltique, effectuer le transport des troupes et pour les communications necessaires.

Article III
S.M.le Roi de Suède et de Norvége s'oblige de fournir pour sa part …hommes de troupes de terre et Batiments de guerre comformement à l'etat ci-joint. S.M.l'Empereur de Français et S.M.la Reine du Royaume Uni de Grande Bretagne et d'Irlande s'engagent à fournir le reste des forces de terre et de mer stipulés dans l'article II.

S.M.l'Empereur de Français et S.M.la Reine du Royaume Uni de Grande Bretagne et d'Irlande promessent en autre de payer à S.M. le Roi de Suède et de Norvége à titre de subsides pendant la durée de la guerre … ? mensuellement et comme frais de mise en campagnes ? cette somme sera liquidée des que les ratifications de la presente convention seront echangés. Les subsides continueront un mois apres la cessation des hostilités pour remmenes les troupes Suèco-Norvègiennes dans leurs payers et remplacer le materiel sesi(?) ou detruit.

Article IV

Un plan de campagne sera concerté et adopté par les hautes parti contractants et apres d'obtenir l'ensemble et l'unité d'action indispensables pour ? des resultats decisifs, la direction suprème des operations militaires, tout sur mer que sur terre, en conformité avec le plan de campagne commun sera confié à S.M.le Roi de Suède et de Norvége . Le commandement immediate de force de terre et de mer de chacune nation demeurera entre les mains des generaux et amiraux designés à cet effet par leur gouvernments respectif.

Article V

La paix avec la Russie sera conclu que d'un commun accord entre les puissances contractés qui en seront les signatoires.

Article VI

Les 4 puissances ? donneront connaissance de la presente convention à la Cour de Danemarc et reçevont avec ? son adhesion dans les conditions suivantes.

Article VII

Le Danemarc s'engage d' ? …. Hommes de terre et Batiment de guerre pour ? à l'accomplissement de l'œuvre mentionée dans l'article Ier. Ces troupes seront placés sous le commandement du Roi de Suède et de Norvége et S.M. l'Empereur de Français ainsi que S. M. la Reine du Royaume Uni de Grande Bretagne et d'Irlande fournir pour la mise en campagne l'entretien et le retour du Corps Danois des payers des subsides proportionels à ceux qui se trouvent stipulés dans l'article III.

Article VIII
S.M.l'Empereur d'Autriche, S.M.l'Empereur de Français, S.M.la Reine du Royaume Uni de Grande Bretagne et d'Irlande et S.M. le Roi de Suède et de Norvége s'engagent à maintenir l'integrité de la monarchie Danoise conforment au traité de Londres de Mai 185 et reconaissent les droits de S.M. Danoise au péage du Sound

[Translation]
Secret clauses
Article I
H.M. the Emperor of Austria, H.M. the Emperor of the French, H.M. the Queen of the United Kingdom of Great Britain and Ireland and H.M. the King of Sweden and Norway, recognising the importance that the weakening of Russia's power in the Baltic Sea and the re-establishment as far as circumstances would permit of the political equilibrium in the North compromised by the aggrandisement of Russia would mean for all of Europe, promise each other a close alliance as well as to unite their efforts to achieve this result.
Article II
H.M. the Emperor of the French, H.M. the Queen of the United Kingdom of Great Britain and Ireland and H.M. the King of Sweden and Norway undertake to put into the field for next spring in order to achieve the aforesaid aim .... soldiers and sufficient naval forces to dominate the Baltic Sea, undertake the troop transports and maintain the necessary communications.
Article III
H.M. the King of Sweden and Norway undertakes for his part to provide .... soldiers and vessels of war in accordance with the joint state. H.M. the Emperor of the French, H.M. the Queen of the United Kingdom of Great Britain and Ireland undertake to provide the rest of the forces on land and sea stipulated in article II.

H.M. the Emperor of the French, H.M. the Queen of the United Kingdom of Great Britain and Ireland promise in addition to pay to H.M. the King of Sweden and Norway as subsidies for the duration of the war .... each month and [?] to defray the cost of preparing for the campaign. This sum will be available as soon as the ratifications of this convention will be exchanged. The subsidies will continue for one month after the cessation of hostilities in order to return the Swedish-Norwegian troops to their countries and to replace material seized or destroyed.

Article IV

A campaign plan will be drawn up and adopted by the high contracting parties and after achieving the overall and united action indispensable to [achieve?] decisive results, the supreme direction of military operations, in conformance with the joint campaign plan, will be entrusted to H.M. the King of Sweden and Norway. The immediate command of each nation's forces of land and sea will remain in the hands of the generals and admirals designated for this purpose by their respective governments.

Article V

Peace with Russia will only be concluded by common accord between the contracting parties which will be the signatories.

Article VI

The 4 [contracting?] powers will inform the Danish Court of this convention and will [?] receive its adhesion under the following conditions.

Article VII

Denmark undertakes to [supply?] .... troops and vessels of war to [support? Enable?] the accomplishment of the undertaking mentioned in the first article. These troops will be placed under the command of H.M the King of Sweden and Norway and H.M. the Emperor of the French as well as H.M. the Queen of the United Kingdom of Great Britain and Ireland supply, in order to put into the field, support and return the Danish Corps to its country, subsidies proportional to those that are stipulated in article III.

Article VIII

H.M. the Emperor of Austria, H.M. the Emperor of the French, H.M. the Queen of the United Kingdom of Great Britain and Ireland and H.M. the King of Sweden and Norway undertake to maintain the integrity of the Danish Monarchy in accordance with the Treaty of London in May 185[?] and recognise H. Danish M.'s right to the Sound tolls.

Note: the last Article refers to the London Protocol signed on 8th May 1852 after the First War of Schleswig. The Protocol affirmed the integrity of the Danish federation as a "European necessity and standing principle". Accordingly, the duchies of Schleswig (a Danish fief), and Holstein and Lauenburg (German fiefs) were joined by personal union with the Kingdom of Denmark. However, Frederick VII of Denmark was childless, so a change in dynasty was imminent and the lines of succession for the duchies and Denmark conflicted. That meant that, contrary to the Protocol, the new King of Denmark would not also be the new duke of Holstein and duke of Lauenburg. So for this purpose, the line of succession to the duchies was modified. Further, it was affirmed that the duchies were to remain as independent entities, and that Schleswig would have no greater constitutional affinity to Denmark than Holstein.[ccclx]

Appendix 4 – King Oscar's plan for the 1856 campaign[ccclxi]

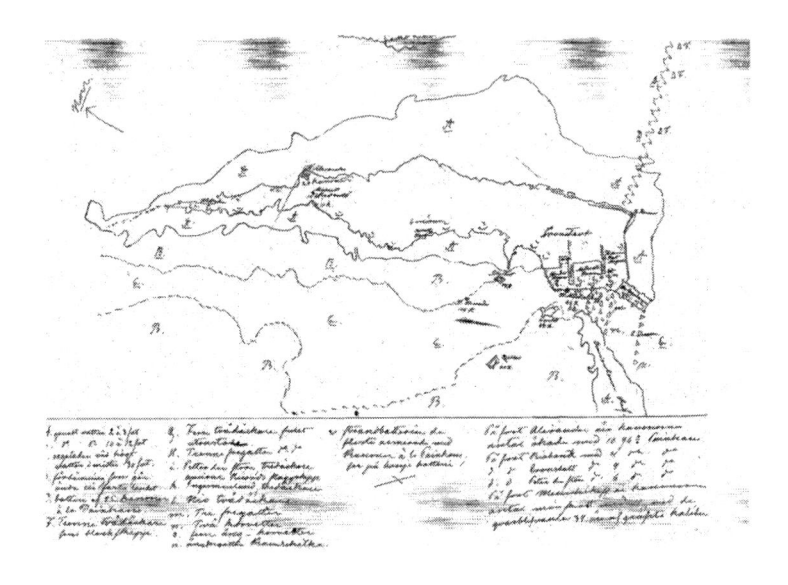

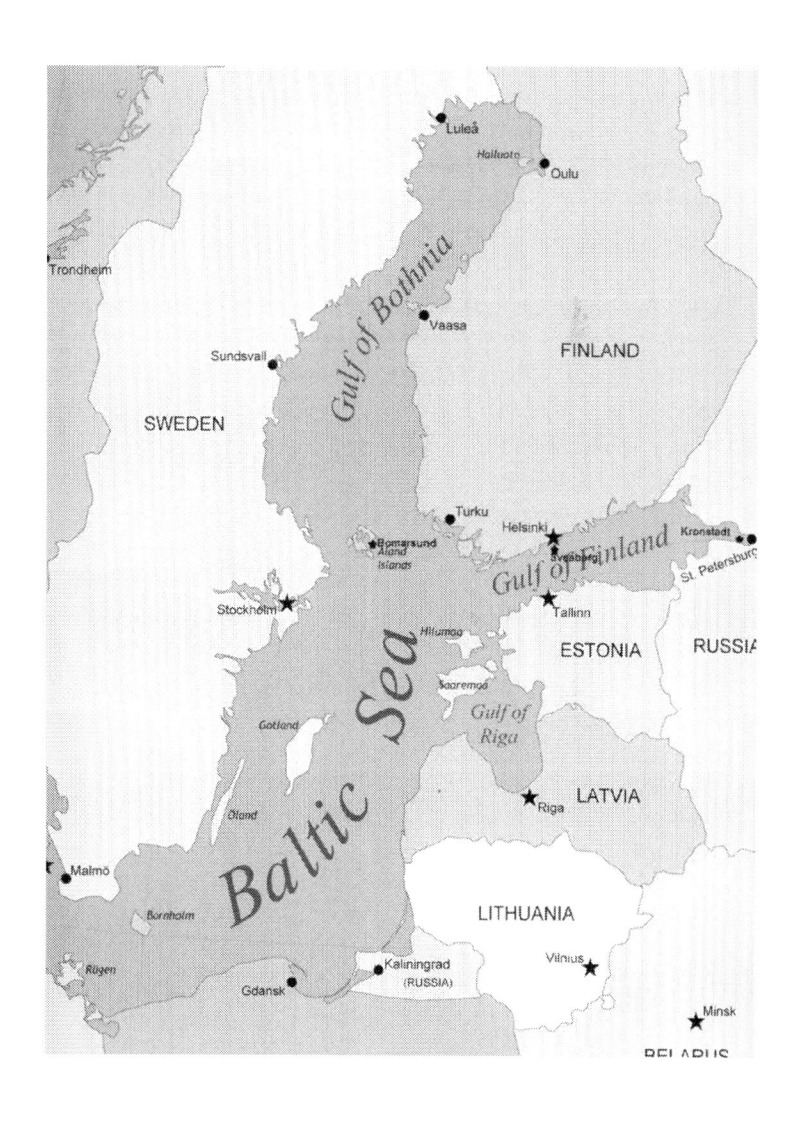

The Baltic[ccclxii]

Endnotes

[i] W C Sellar & R J Yeatman, *1066 and All That*, (London 2005), p. 147

[ii] The following terms will be used: 'Sweden' refers both to that country only, and is used as a short-hand term for the United Kingdoms of Sweden & Norway. This is because most of the relevant issues – internal debate, foreign policy and so on – tended to be Swedish issues. From time to time, the terms the Scandinavian Monarchy or Sweden & Norway will also be used. Norway on its own will only be used for an issue that specifically concerns Norway but not Sweden. Great Britain and Britain will be used interchangeably. 'England' will only be used in direct quotes. 'The Allies' refers to Great Britain and France, even though their alliance included Turkey and – eventually – Sardinia.

[iii] Alexander William Kinglake, *The Invasion of the Crimea: Its origin and an account of its progress down to the death of Lord Raglan*, London, 1863, vol I, p. 458. None of the following words appear in the index covering the eight volumes: Åland, Bomarsund, Sveaborg, Kronstadt (or Cronstadt), Oscar (or Oskar), or Sweden.

[iv] Winston S Churchill, *History of the English-Speaking Peoples*, volume IV, The Great Democracies (London 1958), p. 58

[v] Saul David, *Victoria's Wars* (London 2007), p. 248

[vi] Eg, putting the Church of the Holy Sepulchre in Bethlehem, Trevor Royle, Crimea – *The Great Crimean War*, (London 1999), p. 482; or referring to a British Embassy (rather than legation) in Serbia in the 1850s, p. 179

[vii] Royle, p. 152

[viii] John Shelton Curtiss, *Russia's Crimean War*, Durham, NC, 1979, pp 284, 286, 436.

[ix] Ibid., p. 285

[x] Ibid., p. 288

[xi] Ibid., p. 419

[xii] David Wetzel, *The Crimean War: A Diplomatic History*, New York, 1985

[xiii] Winfried Baumgart, *The Crimean War 1853-1856,* London 2000, p. 43

[xiv] Ibid., p. 45

[xv] Ibid., pp. 43-45

[xvi] Andrew D Lambert, *The Crimean War: British Grand Strategy 1853-1856*, (Manchester 1991), p. xvii

[xvii] Ibid., p. 74.

[xviii] Ibid., p. 6

[xix] Ibid., p. 73

[xx] Lambert, pp. 96, 181

[xxi] Basil Greenhill & Ann Giffard, *The British Assault on Finland 1854-1844 – A Forgotten Naval War,* London, 1988, p. 10

[xxii] Ibid., p. 339

[xxiii] W E Mosse, *The Rise and Fall of the Crimean System 1855-71*, London 1963, p. 22; Axel E Jonasson, The Crimean War, the Beginning of Strict Swedish Neutrality and the Myth

of Swedish Intervention in the Baltic, *Journal of Baltic Studies 4,* 1973, p. 248

[xxiv] Hallendorff, *Oscar I, Napoleon och Nikolaus*, p. 117

[xxv] Edgar Anderson, The Scandinavian Area and the Crimean War in the Baltic, *Scandinavian Studies, 41* (August 1969), p. 265

[xxvi] Anderson, The Scandinavian Area, p. 274

[xxvii] Ibid., p. 264

[xxviii] Anderson, The Crimean War in the Baltic Area, *Journal of Baltic Studies*, 5:4, p. 353; Baumgart, pp 10, 197; Curtiss, p. 499; Greenhill & Giffard, p. 341; Lambert, p. 317; Mosse, *The Rise and Fall*, p. 22

[xxix] Curtiss, p. 479; Greenhill & Giffard, p. 340; Mosse, *The Rise and Fall*, p. 22

[xxx] Lambert, p. 317

[xxxi] Albin Cullberg, *La politique du roi Oscar I pendant la guerre de Crimée : études diplomatiques sur les négociations secrètes entre les cabinets de Stocholm, Paris, Saint Pétersbourg et Londres les années 1853-1856*, (Stockholm 1912), vol 2, p. 37.

[xxxii] Ibid., vol 1, pp 60, 88, vol 2, p. 62

[xxxiii] Cullberg, vol 2, p. 80

[xxxiv] Hallendorff, *Konung Oscar I:s politik under Krimkriget*, Uppsala, 1930, p. 7

[xxxv] Ibid., p. 20

[xxxvi] Sven Eriksson, *Svensk diplomati och tidningspress under Krimkriget*, Stockholm, 1939, p. 293

[xxxvii] C F Palmstierna, *Sverige, Ryssland och England 1833-1855 – Kring novembertraktatens förutsättningar,* PhD thesis, Stockholm 1932, p. 3

[xxxviii] Ibid., p. 11

[xxxix] Carl Michael Runeberg, *Finland under Orientaliska Kriget*, Helsingfors, 1962, p. 162

[xl] Eva Helen Ulvros, *Oscar I – En biografi*, (Stockholm 2007), p.

[xli] Herman Lindqvist, *Historien om Sverige, volym VIII, Ånga och Dynamit*, chapter 5. For criticism of Lindqvist, see eg, Peter Englund's review Herman snubblar, September, 1994 www.peterenglund.com/textarkiv/lindqvistbok.htm

[xlii] Carl Michael Runeberg, *Sveriges politik under Krimkriget, Neutralitetsförklaringen 1853-1854*, PhD thesis, Ekenäs, 1934, p. 139

[xliii] Eriksson, p. 24

[xliv] Eg, Royle, p. 152; Curtiss, p. 288; Lambert, p. 96

[xlv] Wetzel, p. 28

[xlvi] Baumgart, p. 6

[xlvii] Palmstierna, pp 13-14

[xlviii] Ibid., p. 11, 87

[xlix] Curtiss, p. 16

[i] Curtiss, p. 73

[ii] Ibid., p. 77

[iii] Royle, p. 19

[iiii] Ibid., p. 19

[iv] David, p. 175

[v] Ibid., p. 175, Royle p. 20

[vi] Ibid., vol I, p. 89

[vii] Curtiss, p. 81

[viii] Kinglake, p. 96

[ix] Eriksson, p. 65

[x] Ibid., p. 65; Curtiss, p. 148

[xi] Royle, p. 34

[xii] Hallendorff, *Oscar I, Napoleon och Nikolaus – ur diplomaternas privata brev under Krimkriget,* Stockholm, 1918, p. 164

[xiii] Wetzel, p. 114

[xiv] Ibid., p. 114; Royle, p. 455

[xv] Quoted in Hallendorff *Oscar I, Napoleon och Nikolaus*, p. 21

[xvi] Baumgart, p. 30

[xvii] Baum, p. 30

[xviii] Kinglake, p. 484

[lxix] The Right Hon Sir Herbert Maxwell, *The Life and Letters of George William Frederick Fourth Earl of Clarendon, KG, GCB*, London 1913, p. 73

[lxx] Baumgart, p. 6

[lxxi] Baumgart, p. 16

[lxxii] Curtiss, p. 217

[lxxiii] Baumgart, p. 35

[lxxiv] Ibid., p. 6

[lxxv] Ibid., p. 27

[lxxvi] Royle, p. 310

[lxxvii] Curtiss, p. 398, Runeberg *Finland under Orientaliska kriget,* p. 113

[lxxviii] Runeberg, *Finland under Orientaliska kriget*, p. 96

[lxxix] Carl Michael Runeberg, *Sveriges politik under Krimkriget,* p. 63f

[lxxx] Palmstierna, p. 19

[lxxxi] Hallendorff, *Kung Oscar I:s politik*, p. 5

[lxxxii] Jansson, p. 217

[lxxxiii] Ibid., p. 195

[lxxxiv] Jansson, p. 195

[lxxxv] Jansson, p. 196

[lxxxvi] Palmstierna, p. 42

[lxxxvii] Scandinavism was a popular movement and occasional policy aimed at closer cooperation between the three Scandinavian peoples (Swedes, Danes and Norwegians). It flourished in the middle decades of the 19th Century. At one stage, Scandinavists hoped that the either King Frederik VI of Denmark might gain the Swedish throne in 1809; or that King Frederik VII of Denmark, who was childless, might adopt the Swedish Crown Prince Karl and unite the three Kingdoms in the mid-19th Century. Russia's predominance in the Baltic meant that Scandinavism – which included references to the lost brethren in Finland - was a potentially hostile force. See Lindqvist, chapters 3 and 5.

[lxxxviii] Palmstierna, p. 51

[lxxxix] Palmstierna, p. 18

[xc] Ibid., p. 11

[xci] Eriksson, p. 7

[xcii] Palmstierna, pp 87-158

[xciii] Jansson, p. 519; Lindqvist, p. 169. A slightly different total – 157,368 – is given in *Sammandrag öfver Svenska Arméens personal och hästar samt den, försvarsverket till lands tillhöriga, materiel, ny, brukbar eller reparabel som kan ifrågakomma att användas vid en möjlig förestående krigsrustning. Förhållandet år 1850-51* (*Summary of the Swedish army's personnel and horses and material belonging to the defence forces on land, new, useable or capable of being repaired, that can be used at a possibly incipient armament for war. The situation in 1850-51*) dated 21st March, 1852, Bernadotte Family Archive, Karl XV (BFA KXV), volume 14

[xciv] Jansson, p. 459

[xcv] Ibid., p. 397

[xcvi] Baumgart, p. 63; Curtiss, p. 460

[xcvii] Baumgart, p. 168, BFA Oscar I & Josefina (OI&J), volume 36; Cullberg, vol I, p. 36

[xcviii] Jansson, p. 374; FO 73/274 48, Arthur Magenis to Lord Clarendon; BFA KXV vol 15

[xcix] BFA OI&J, vol 48, the number refers to 1856

[c] Jansson, p. 328

[ci] Ibid., p. 328

[cii] Ibid., p. 191

[ciii] Ibid., p. 289

[civ] Runeberg, *Finland under Orientaliska Kriget*, p. 9

[cv] Royle, p. 65

[cvi] Greenhill & Giffard, p. 82; Earp, pp 41, 42; Eriksson, p. 155

[cvii] C I Hamilton, Sir James Graham, the Baltic Campaign and War-Planning at the Admiralty in 1854, *The Historical Journal*, 19, Cambridge, 1976 (JSTOR), p. 112

[cviii] Ibid., p. 92

[cix] Jansson, p. 217

[cx] Eriksson, pp 15, 16

[cxi] Runeberg, *Sveriges politik under Krimkriget*, p. 146

[cxii] Quoted in Axel E Jonasson, The Crimean War, the Beginning of Strict Swedish Neutrality and the Myth of Swedish Intervention in the Baltic, *Journal of Baltic Studies 4,* 1973, p. 248

[cxiii] Royle, p. 66

[cxiv] Eg, Ulvros p. 252

[cxv] Jansson, p. 366

[cxvi] Eg, BFA OI&J, vol 36, notes from an audience for the French Minister Lobstein; and diary notes from 12th July, 1855

[cxvii] Runeberg, *Sveriges politik*, p. 372

[cxviii] Runeberg, *Sveriges politik*, p. 67

[cxix] Eg, Royle, p. 152

[cxx] Eriksson, p. 77; TNA FO 73/254 no 17, 25th August, 1853

[cxxi] Runeberg, *Finland under Orientaliska Kriget*, p. 14

[cxxii] Ibid., pp 372-373

[cxxiii] Earp, p. 35; Williams, p. 265

[cxxiv] Palmstierna, p. 42

[cxxv] Ibid., pp 51, 56

[cxxvi] Runeberg, *Sveriges politik under Krimkriget*, p. 184

[cxxvii] Ibid., p. 184

[cxxviii] Ibid., p. 188

[cxxix] Ibid., p. 188

[cxxx] Runeberg, *Sveriges politik*, p. 185 ff

[cxxxi] Ibid., p. 185 ff.

[cxxxii] Ibid., p. 247

[cxxxiii] Ibid., p. 247

[cxxxiv] Ibid., p. 256

[cxxxv] Ibid., p. 216

[cxxxvi] Runeberg, *Sveriges politik under Krimkriget*, p. 214

[cxxxvii] Ibid., pp 211-213

[cxxxviii] Runeberg, *Sveriges politik under Krimkriget*, pp 215, 262

[cxxxix] Eriksson, p. 90

[cxl] Hallendorff, *Oscar I, Napoleon och Nikolaus*, p. 153

[cxli] UD 21 F vol 1104, Dispatch from the Swedish Minister Baron Rehausen to the Prime Minister for Foreign Affairs Baron Stierneld

[cxlii] Runeberg, *Sveriges politik*, p. 384

[cxliii] Axel E Jonasson, The Crimean War, the Beginning of Strict Swedish Neutrality and the Myth of Swedish Intervention in the Baltic, *Journal of Baltic Studies 4,* 1973, p. 245

[cxliv] Runeberg, *Sveriges politik*, p. 263

[cxlv] Runeberg, *Sveriges politik*, pp 271-272; However, Eriksson (p. 128), believes that the last point is the King's embellishment, as Dashkov's own report does not contain anything on the different treatment of the Swedish and Danish notes.

[cxlvi] Eriksson, p. 139

[cxlvii] Runeberg, *Sveriges politik*, p. 351

[cxlviii] Runeberg, *Sveriges politik.*, p. 355

[cxlix] Ibid., p. 360

[cl] UD HA A3A vol 7

[cli] Eg, Eriksson, p. 25

[clii] Ibid., pp 22-24

[cliii] Runeberg, *Sveriges politik*, p. 141

[cliv] Eriksson, p. 68

[clv] Runeberg, *Sveriges politik*, p. 147

[clvi] Runeberg, *Sveriges politik.*, p. 281

[clvii] Eriksson, p. 120

[clviii] See, eg, Benson & Esher (eds), *The Letters of Queen Victoria: A Selection of Her Majesty's Correspondence between the Years 1836 and 1861, volumes III*, London 1908, letter from the Earl of Aberdeen to Queen Victoria, p. 48; and from Queen Victoria to Lord Clarendon, p. 51

[clix] Royle, p. 43

[clx] Charles Stuart Parker, *Life and letters of Sir James Graham, Second Baronet of Netherby*, London 1907, vol II, p. 223

[clxi] Royle, p. 152

[clxii] Lambert, p. 73

[clxiii] Runeberg, *Finland under Orientaliska Kriget*, p. 25; National Archives, Foreign Office 73 (Correspondence with Sweden), 259, henceforth TNA FO 73/259, no 60

[clxiv] B Earp (ed) *The History of the Baltic Campaign of 1854. From documents and other materials furnished by Vice-Admiral Sir Charles Napier*. London 1857, p. 57

[clxv] Ibid., p. 69

[clxvi] Earp, p. 86

[clxvii] PRO 30/22/11D, Lord John Russell papers, no 56, 20th May, 1854

[clxviii] Earp, p. 18

[clxix] Ibid., p. 7

[clxx] Ibid., p. 35

[clxxi] Ibid., p. 41f

[clxxii] Cullberg, vol I, p. 76

[clxxiii] Runeberg, *Finland under Orientaliska Kriget*, p. 27

[clxxiv] Hugh Noel Williams, *The Life and letters of Admiral Sir Charles Napier K.C.B.*, London 1917, p. 245

[clxxv] Greenhill & Giffard, p. 198

[clxxvi] Runeberg, *Finland under Orientaliska Kriget*, p. 18

[clxxvii] Parker, vol II, p. 231; D Bonner-Smith & A C Dewar (eds), *Russian War, 1854, Baltic and Black Sea: official correspondence*, London 1943, p. 13

[clxxviii] Lambert, p. 165

[clxxix] Greenhill & Giffard quote King Oscar as calling the destruction on the Finnish coast "barbarous and unworthy of our time", p. 171; they also refer to articles in *The Times* reporting the negative reaction in Sweden to the raids, p. 181. However, a letter from Sir William Grey to Lord Clarendon (FO 73/262, # 239) contradicts this. Grey quotes King Oscar as saying that saying that those who compare the British raids this to the Sinope Massacre are fools, the measures had been severe but that they were necessary and that the King was convinced it would turn the Finns against Russia. But Grey's report is hearsay, based on what he was told by an unnamed source who had had an audience with the King.

[clxxx] Runeberg, *Finland under Orientaliska Kriget*, p. 29

[clxxxi] Eg, online on http://www.histdoc.net/history/fr/frhamn.html in Swedish, Finnish and Russian

[clxxxii] Palmstierna, p. 26

[clxxxiii] Earp, p127.

[clxxxiv] Hamilton, p. 92

[clxxxv] Jonasson, p. 247; Runeberg, *Finland under Orientaliska Kriget,* pp 22, 31

[clxxxvi] Williams, p. 288

[clxxxvii] Bonner-Smith & Dewar, p. 13; Royle, p. 163

[clxxxviii] Greenhill & Giffard, p. 121; Anderson *The Crimean War in the Baltic Area*, p. 354; Curtiss, p. 439

[clxxxix] Hallendorff, *Konung Oscar I:s politik*, p. 7

[cxc] J B Conacher, *Britain and the Crimea: Problems of War and Peace*, London 1987, p. 423

[cxci] Baumgart, p. 43

[cxcii] Eriksson, p. 183

[cxciii] Runeberg, *Finland under Orientaliska Kriget*, p. 50. The date is unclear, but Virgin was only Minister from 24th March to 11th September 1854. The Neutrality Declaration entered into force on 8th April, 1854.

[cxciv] Ibid., p. 50

[cxcv] BFA, OI & J vol 36 Oscar I *Anteckningar från åren 1854-1856* (Notes from the years 1854-1856).

[cxcvi] Greenhill & Giffard, p. 195

[cxcvii] Earp, pp 41, 42; Runeberg, *Finland under Orientaliska Kriget*, pp 27, 29; Williams, p. 303; Eriksson, p. 155

[cxcviii] Earp, pp 124, 126

[cxcix] Ibid., p. 124

[cc] Hallendorff, *Oscar I, Napoleon och Nikolaus*, p. 44

[cci] Eriksson, p. 184

[ccii] Eriksson, p. 188

[cciii] BFA, OI & J vol 36 *Anteckningar*; Eriksson, p. 189

[cciv] TNA PRO 30/22/11 D, Lord john Russell Memorandum, 20th May 1854

[ccv] TNA, PRO 30/22/11D, #70 Cabinet Members' comments on Lord John Russell Memo

[ccvi] Ibid., #68

[ccvii] Ibid., #60

[ccviii] Ibid., #78

[ccix] Ibid., #80

[ccx] Ibid., #96

[ccxi] BFA, OI & J vol 36 *Anteckningar*

[ccxii] Runeberg, *Finland under Orientaliska Kriget*, pp. 74-77

[ccxiii] Runeberg, *Finland under Orientaliska Kriget*, p. 84

[ccxiv] Hallendorff, *Oscar I, Napoleon och Nikolaus*, p. 44

[ccxv] TNA FO 73/262, #239, Grey to Clarendon, 22nd June, 1854

[ccxvi] Hallendorff, *Oscar I, Napoleon och Nikolaus*, p. 212

[ccxvii] TNA FO 73/262, Grey to Clarendon, 27th June, 1854

[ccxviii] Runeberg, *Finland under Orientaliska Kriget*, p. 91

[ccxix] Eriksson, p. 196; TNA FO 72/262, #292

[ccxx] TNA FO 73/262 #289, Grey to Clarendon, 24th July, 1854; Eriksson, p. 196; Runeberg, *Finland under Orientaliska Kriget*, p. 105

[ccxxi] Eriksson, p. 196; Runeberg, *Finland under Orientaliska Kriget*, p. 109

[ccxxii] Cullberg, vol I, p. 79

[ccxxiii] Mansbach was Norwegian, one of the few Norwegians to reach the top of the United Kingdoms' diplomatic service.

[ccxxiv] Runeberg, *Finland under Orientaliska Kriget*, p. 100

[ccxxv] Runeberg, *Finland under Orientaliska Kriget*, p. 101

[ccxxvi] Ibid., p. 101

[ccxxvii] Ibid., p. 110

[ccxxviii] Ibid., p. 102

[ccxxix] Runeberg, *Finland under Orientaliska Kriget*, p. 125

[ccxxx] Ibid., p. 178

[ccxxxi] Ibid., p. 134

[ccxxxii] Ibid., p. 151

[ccxxxiii] Runeberg, *Finland under Orientaliska Kriget*, p. 159; BFA OI & J, vol 36 *Anteckningar*

[ccxxxiv] Hallendorff, *Oscar I, Napoleon och Nikolaus*, p. 41f

[ccxxxv] Eriksson, p 206. Eriksson assumes that the article was 'inspired' by the Swedish court.

[ccxxxvi] BFA OI & J, vol 36, *Anteckningar*; Hallendorff, *Oscar I, Napoleon och Nikolaus*, p. 53

[ccxxxvii] Hallendorff, *Oscar I, Napoleon och Nikolaus*, p. 51

[ccxxxviii] Cullberg, vol I, p. 75

[ccxxxix] Eriksson, p. 210

[ccxl] Eriksson, p. 210

[ccxli] Runeberg, *Finland under Orientaliska Kriget*, p. 25

[ccxlii] BFA, OI & J, vol 47

[ccxliii] TNA FO 73/259, #22;

[ccxliv] Hallendorff, *Konung Oscar I:s politik*, p. 55

[ccxlv] Runeberg, *Finland under Orientaliska Kriget*, p. 160

[ccxlvi] Ibid., p. 113

[ccxlvii] Hallendorff, *Oscar I, Napoleon och Nikolaus*, p. 68

[ccxlviii] Walewski was the illegitimate son of the Emperor Napoleon I and thus Napoleon III's cousin. He would later succeed Droyun de Lhuys as his cousin's Foreign Minister.

[ccxlix] Riksarkivet Utrikesdepartementet (Swedish National Archive, Foreign Office), 1 O, vol 48

[ccl] Bonner-Smith, p. 5

[ccli] Greenhill & Giffard, p. 296

[cclii] John Campbell, Marquis of Lorne, Viscount Palmerston KG, London 1892, p. 169
[ccliii] Baumgart, p. 168

[ccliv] Anderson, The Crimean War in the Baltic Area, p. 348

[cclv] Cullberg, vol II, p. 21

[cclvi] Quoted in Royle, p. 379

[cclvii] Baumgart, p. 174

[cclviii] Royle, p. 382; Lambert, p. 287

[cclix] Bonner-Smith, p. 271

[cclx] Baumgart, p. 175; Greenhill & Giffard, p. 296

[cclxi] Cullberg, vol II, p. 25

[cclxii] Posthumus (Johan Carl Hellberg), *Ur minnet och dagboken om Mina Samtida, Personer och Händelser efter 1815 inom och utom Fäderneslandet, 7-8*, Stockholm, 1871, p. 101; *Helsingfors Morgonbladet*, no 63, 20th August, 1855; *Wiborg* no 67, 24th August, 1855 and no 68, 28th August 1855

[cclxiii] Baumgart, p. 173

[cclxiv] Ibid. p. 174

[cclxv] BFA KXV, vol. 15

[cclxvi] BFA O1&J, vol. 48. The number is for early 1856

[cclxvii] Anderson, The Crimean War in the Baltic Area, p. 354

[cclxviii] Cullberg, vol II, p. 88

[cclxix] Barck had among other things arranged a passport for the then pretender Louis-Napoleon when the latter wanted to visit Paris shortly after the February Revolution. Hallendorff, *Oscar I, Napoleon och Nikolaus*, p. 84

[cclxx] Hallendorff, *Oscar I, Napoleon och Nikolaus*, p. 87

[cclxxi] Eriksson, p. 247

[cclxxii] Cullberg, vol I, p. 40

[cclxxiii] Eriksson, p. 250

[cclxxiv] Cullberg, vol II, p. 47

[cclxxv] Ibid., p. 47

[cclxxvi] Hallendorff, *Oscar I, Napoleon och Nikolaus*, p. 88

[cclxxvii] Hallendorff, *Oscar I, Napoleon och Nikolaus*, p. 90

[cclxxviii] Baumgart, p. 19

[cclxxix] Ibid., p. 19

[cclxxx] BFA OI&J vol 36

[cclxxxi] Ibid.

[cclxxxii] Ibid.

[cclxxxiii] Ibid.

[cclxxxiv] Hallendorff, *Oscar I, Napoleon och Nikolaus*, p. 111

[cclxxxv] Palmstierna, p. 381

[cclxxxvi] Palmstierna, p. 381f

[cclxxxvii] Manderström had mentioned the issue of ice-free ports in Varangerfiord and that Russia might seize them to Grey in January 1854. Eriksson, p. 145

[cclxxxviii] BFA OI&J vol 36

[cclxxxix] Ibid.

[ccxc] Palmstierna, p. 385; Eriksson, eg., Chapter X, p. 145ff

[ccxci] A G Jomini. *Étude diplomatique sur la Guerre de Crimée, par Un Ancien Diplomat*, St Petersburg, 1878, p. 368

[ccxcii] Cullberg, vol II, p. 85

[ccxciii] Ibid., vol I, p. 20

[ccxciv] Palmstierna, p. 369

[295] Eriksson, p. 153

[296] TNA FO 73-270, #79

[297] Cullberg, vol II, p. 53

[298] Ibid., vol II p. 53 The exact dates of these meetings are somewhat unclear. Hallendorff (*Kung Oscar I:s politik,* p. 66)claims that the King saw Magenis on the 10th and Lobstein on the 15th. King Oscar's own notes are written on 19th July, but here too Lobstein's audience is said to have been the day after Magenis'.

[299] Jonasson, p. 248

[300] Eriksson, p. 268

[301] TNA FO 881/494

[302] Eriksson, p. 271

[303] UD 1 O, vol 48

[304] Hallendorff, *Oscar I, Napoleon och Nikolaus*, p. 91

[305] Lambert, p. 301

[306] TNA FO 73/270, #184

[307] Palmstierna, p. 380

[308] Benson & Esher, vol III, p. 133

[309] TNA FO 73/271, #204

[310] Hallendorff, *Kung Oscar I:s politik*, p. 65f

[311] Eriksson, p. 276

[cccxii] Hallendorff, *Kung Oscar I:s politik*, p. 71-72

[cccxiii] Hallendorff, *Kung Oscar I:s politik*, p. 72

[cccxiv] Eg., Royle, p. 445

[cccxv] Hallendorff, *Oscar I, Napoleon och Nikolaus,* p. 117

[cccxvi] Posthumus, vol VII, pp. 102-103

[cccxvii] Hallendorff, *Kung Oscar I:s politik*, p. 85

[cccxviii] BFA OI&J, vol 36; Hallendorff, *Kung Oscar I:s politik*, pp. 86-96

[cccxix] Hallendorff, *Kung Oscar I:s politik*, p. 86

[cccxx] TNA FO 73/271, #270, Magenis to Clarendon 29th October

[cccxxi] Hallendorff, *Kung Oscar I:s politik*, p. 73

[cccxxii] TNA FO 73/271, #281

[cccxxiii] TNA FO 73/271, #307

[cccxxiv] RA UD 1 O vol 48

[cccxxv] BFA OI&J vol 48

[cccxxvi] Lambert, p. 301

[cccxxvii] Posthumus, vol VII, p. 110

[cccxxviii] Greenhill & Giffard, p. 340

[cccxxix] Mosse, p. 22; Jonasson, p. 248

[cccxxx] Hallendorff, *Oscar I, Napoleon och Nikolaus*, p. 354

[cccxxxi] Lambert, p. 317

[cccxxxii] BFA OI&J vol 48

[cccxxxiii] Palmstierna, p. 359

[cccxxxiv] BFA OI&J vol 36

[cccxxxv] Eriksson, p. 353

[cccxxxvi] Hallendorff, *Kung Oscar I:s politik*, p. 105

[cccxxxvii] Palmstierna, p. 367

[cccxxxviii] Eriksson, p. 355

[cccxxxix] Ibid., p 357

[cccxl] Ibid., p 367

[cccxli] Eg., Baumgart, p. 165; Benson & Esher, p. 156 (Palmerston writing to Queen Victoria about plans for 1856); Royle, p. 385

[cccxlii] Hallendorff, *Oscar I, Napoleon och Nikolaus*, p. 92

[cccxliii] Hallendorff, *Oscar I, Napoleon och Nikolaus*, p. 13

[cccxliv] Hallendorff, *Kung Oscar I:s politik*, p. 115

[cccxlv] Ibid., p 115

[cccxlvi] Ulvros, p. 252

[cccxlvii] Hallendorff, *Oscar I, Napoleon och Nikolaus, p. 118*

[cccxlviii] Eg., Baumgart, p. 197f; Lambert, p. 298; Mosse, pp. 24, 25, 29; Jonasson, p. 250

[cccxlix] Anderson, The Crimean War in the Baltic Area, p. 339

[cccl] Eg., Hallendorff, Oscar I, Napoleon och Nikolaus, p. 399

[cccli] Eriksson, p. 375

[ccclii] Eriksson, pp. 297, 302

[cccliii] Runeberg, Finland under Orientaliska Kriget, p. 105

[cccliv] Eriksson, p. 338

[ccclv] Eg., Runeberg, Finland under Orientaliska Krigte, p. 111

[ccclvi] Jonasson, p. 250

[ccclvii] TNA FO 881/714

[ccclviii] RA UD 1 O vol 48

[ccclix] BFA OI&J vol 48

[ccclx]

[ccclxi] BFA OI&J vol 37

[ccclxii] Downloaded from Wikipedia (www.wikipedia.org)

Printed in Great Britain
by Amazon